The Great Trek

NEW FOOTSTEPS ON THE OLD MORMON TRAIL

EDITED BY
Don C. Woodward

WRITTEN BY
Twila Van Leer, and staff

PHOTOGRAPHY BY
Jeffrey D. Allred, and staff

Deseret News

SALT LAKE CITY, UTAH

PUBLISHER *Wm. James Mortimer*   EDITOR *John Hughes*

TABLE OF CONTENTS

FOREWORD

Throughout the world, members of The Church of Jesus Christ of Latter-day Saints commemorated the sesquicentennial of the arrival of pioneers into the Valley of the Great Salt Lake. Plays, musicals, dances, songfests and reprises of pioneer wagon trains took place on five continents, including a handcart that originated in Siberia and made its way throughout Russia and Ukraine. Members in 20,000 Church units contributed an estimated 3 million or more hours of service to their communities worldwide.

In all this, the observance that fired the imaginations of hundreds of thousands was the re-enactment of the original pioneer trek by Mormon Trail Wagon Train — 150 Years Inc.

When a small group of history buffs and adventurers began assembling a real wagon train to mark the 150 years since Brigham Young led his people into the lonely valleys of Utah, they had no idea how big a venture it would become — or how real it would be. By the time the wagons, handcarts, outriders and walkers came wearily to the end of their trek they had become front

Framed by a canvas wagon cover, a rider plods with the wagon train as it wends its way along Coyote Creek, approaching the Utah/Wyoming border in July, 1997.

page news and touched the emotions of thousands. Some 220 of the trekkers came the whole distance of more than 1,100 miles. However, an estimated 10,000 people actually took part in the trek. Some came for a day, others for several weeks, but all wanted to feel the dust, sweat, cold and weariness that the original pioneers endured.

This book is a compilation of highlights of the trek as reported in the Deseret News and Church News. It is not the definitive account of the trail, which the newspaper chronicled in its earlier book, "111 Days to Zion." However, through outstanding photographs and articles, it captures the essence of what it feels like to be on a 19th century wagon train driven by a higher purpose.

We made a key decision to begin the story earlier in Nauvoo, Ill., where the sesquicentennial commemoration began in 1996. The story then resumes in the spring of 1997 in Nebraska. We hope that those who took part in the adventure, or who were moved by the link that it made with the past, will accept it as our tribute to their dedication and perseverance.

I

INTRODUCTION

For three months in the summer of 1997 an intrigued world watched as modern pioneers retraced the path of the mid-1800s migration of The Church of Jesus Christ of Latter-day Saints to the Great Basin. The church's hegira to escape persecution in the Midwest has no parallel in American history. Its influence on the settlement of the West was profound and lasting.

From Feb. 4, 1846, when the first wave of church members was driven from Nauvoo, Ill., until May 10, 1869, when the railroad lines from the eastern and western reaches of the country were joined at Promontory, Utah, between 60,000 and 70,000 pioneers plodded along the Mormon Trail. They were driven by religious zeal and the call of church leaders to gather in the Rocky Mountains. Some 6,000 died and were buried along the way, a stark testament to the challenges of the undertaking.

When the rail lines were linked, it essentially ended the use of the trail as the route to "Zion." Portions of the trail became highways, other parts disappeared into cities and suburbs, but a substantial portion remained, the ruts still visible after more than a century.

Sesquicentennial observations of the westward trek began on a bitterly cold day in 1996 in Nauvoo, Ill., with a commemoration of the start of the exodus. Those observances continued in the summer with a commemorative crossing from Nauvoo, on the east bank of the Mississippi River, and a trek to Council Bluffs on the eastern banks of the Missouri River in Iowa — a distance of some 300 miles.

The more ambitious 1997 re-creation memorialized the remainder of the trail from Winter Quarters to the Salt Lake Valley, approximately 1,100 miles.

For many Latter-day Saints, the re-enactments were a link with the past, an opportunity to remember pioneer ancestors who paved the way to a permanent home for the church, now grown to a worldwide organization with some 10 million members. But significantly, hundreds of thousands of people who had no ties to the church avidly followed the re-enactments. They were tangible reminders of the romantic Wild West — an aura that has lingered as part of American lore. Several threads were woven into one cord to bring the re-enactments about. Logistically, they were complex undertakings.

Two groups in Iowa planned commemorative pioneer marches in conjunction with the state's sesquicentennial observance in 1996: JL2, a company formed by a group of Iowa history buffs, and the Iowa Mormon Trails Association, an organization of trail enthusiasts with chapters in 12 counties. The two wagon trains embarked from Nauvoo on June 17, crossing the Mississippi River on a flatboat to Montrose, Iowa, and following the same route but with different schedules for travel and encampments. Three and a half weeks of community activities along the way memorialized several historic moments in the flight of the Latter-day Saints across what was then Iowa Territory. A pause for reflection at the site where William Clayton wrote the beloved pioneer hymn "Come, Come Ye Saints" and re-creation of the Mormon Battalion mustering-in attracted thousands of spectators.

A family moment: Wagon train President Brian Hill shares the triumph with daughter Kalli, 4, as the train pulls into This is the Place State Park.

Meanwhile, several groups, including the two in Iowa, considered plans to commemorate the longer reach of the trail from Winter Quarters to the Salt Lake Valley as part of the 1997 sesquicentennial celebration. The LDS Church had become involved to a degree in the 1996 re-enactment. LDS public affairs missionaries, stake authorities and mission leaders in Iowa mobilized some of their resources to assist the groups as they trekked across the state. The church, however, chose to remain in a supportive role rather than sponsor a 1997 re-enactment.

The Iowa Mormon Trails Association wanted to continue the trek and was joined by its sister association in Nebraska. In Salt Lake City, the family of Robert E. Lowe, owner of the Colorado Stables, had been planning for several years to sponsor a commemorative trek. President Brian Hill of the Kearney Nebraska LDS Stake was called to coordinate the church's involvement.

As these disparate groups communicated, it became apparent that a joint effort could have the greatest impact and the best chance for success. Wagonmasters were selected for the three states over which the 1997 re-enactment would cross: Joe Vogel in Nebraska, Ben Kern in Wyoming and Lowe in Utah. Russ Leger continued to head the Iowa contingent. They began the enormous task of scouting a route that would follow as closely as possible the original Mormon Trail, identifying paths that could be traveled and obtaining permits to cross private and federal lands.

By January 1997, the need for a strong central organization was apparent. A not-for-profit company, Mormon Trail Wagon Train — 150 Years Inc. — was formed with Hill as chief executive. Other members were Leon Wilkinson, operations officer; Stewart Glazier, secretary; Robert S. Clark, attorney; and Brenda L. Cornell, Mike Nelson and Jim Bell, trustees. An advisory committee included the four state wagonmasters, Darlene Hutchison of LDS Public Affairs and Gordon Lowe.

Registration began in earnest. Eventually an estimated 10,000 people were involved in the trek, whether they came for a day, a week or for the duration. Hundreds of groups took advantage of the opportunity to walk in the pioneer footsteps.

The 1997 wagon train departed from two locations. The main company left from historic Winter Quarters near Omaha, Neb., and followed a northern route blazed by Brigham Young's vanguard group of 1847. Another group, consisting mainly of IMTA participants, left from Council Bluffs, Iowa, and followed a more southerly trail used by later groups of Mormon emigrants. The two factions merged at Kearney, Neb., and traveled together the rest of the way to Salt Lake City.

The three-month journey attracted immediate worldwide media attention from the first "wagons, ho!" in Winter Quarters on April 21 to the final thunderous welcome in Salt Lake City on July 22.

4

Utahn Dixon Ford brought his red oxen, Tab and Barr, to Henefer, Utah to join the wagon train for its last few days on the trail.

5

Nature dished up a variety of weather along the trail — just as it had 150 years ago. Here, in eastern Nebraska, dirt roads soon turned to muddy ribbons on a misty day.

PART ONE

NAUVOO:
IN THE BEGINNING

Nauvoo. The name in Hebrew suggests "beautiful place of rest," and the Latter-day Saints under Joseph Smith's leadership worked diligently to make it so. In less than seven years, they turned a tract of Mississippi River swampland on the Illinois-Iowa border into an orderly municipality rivaling Chicago in size.

But by 1846, Mormonism's enemies had destroyed the peace that Joseph Smith meant in naming the city "Nauvoo." In order for the church that he founded to survive, its members knew they must strive to fulfill his prophecy: They would become a mighty people in the Rocky Mountains. Gazing westward across the river and contemplating the daunting journey before them, the Saints must have felt keen trepidation, mitigated by the conviction expressed in the line William Clayton would soon put to music: "We'll find the place which God for us prepared, far away in the West."

Nauvoo today is a small, typically Midwestern town distinguished by a historic district of homes and shops painstakingly restored to reflect 19th century life and pay homage to its original residents. There, in February 1996, the sesquicentennial observance of the Mormon pioneer epoch began, as hundreds met in unbearably cold weather to commemorate the beginning of the trek. The commemoration foreshadowed wagon trek re-enactments that would depart from Nauvoo in June 1996 and culminate in Salt Lake City in July 1997.

IN NAVUOO, A FROZEN EXODUS DOWN THE 'TRAIL OF TEARS'

Tension gripped Nauvoo, Ill., in late 1845. The previous year, on June 27, the LDS Prophet Joseph Smith was murdered by a mob in nearby Carthage. Now, the residents were under virtual siege from arson, assaults and slander.

At a fall conference, church leaders announced the Saints should be ready to depart for the West the following spring, "when the grass grows and the water runs." In ensuing months, the city became a giant wagon-making workshop.

At the same time, residents worked feverishly to complete the Nauvoo Temple, with a portion of it dedicated in time for some 5,600 church members — many of the city's population — to receive ordinances of salvation within its walls. This was viewed as essential to give them the spiritual strength and commitment to withstand the rigors of the westward journey.

By January 1846, rumors and threats were so worrisome that church leaders decided to leave earlier than planned in a small company,

The pioneers of 1846 lit bonfires to fend off freezing cold as they were forced out of Nauvoo. Bonfires were lit across Iowa in 1996 commemorating the events 150 years later.

including as many who wanted to come, with the rest to follow in the spring as originally contemplated.

President Brigham Young, delayed by temple work, was not the first to leave. That distinction fell to Charles Shumway and his family. On Feb. 4, 1846, his wagons and livestock were ferried on a flatboat across the Mississippi River to Montrose, Iowa. In subsequent weeks that winter, some 3,000 frightened exiles followed, huddling in tents at Sugar Creek as they readied themselves to cross the muddy plains of Iowa. Another 10,000 left in the spring. In the fall, mobsters forced out a few hundred poor, sick stragglers, looted the city and desecrated the temple.

Bundled against bitter February cold, 1996 participants march to the riverside for Nauvoo program.

Shumway's departure was commemorated in Nauvoo the weekend of Feb. 3-4, 1996. In a subdued pilgrimage, hundreds of people walked down Parley Street — the "trail of tears" — to the historic ferry landing on the frozen Mississippi. Record-setting cold, with a wind-chill temperature of 50 degrees below zero, was regarded as a harsh reminder of what the Nauvoo Saints suffered.

In a tent warmed only to freezing by space heaters, spectators listened to speeches from historians and church and government officials. The night of Feb. 3, bonfires blazed in more than a dozen communities along the Mormon Trail in Iowa and Nebraska in remembrance that 150 years previously, Nauvoo residents were preparing to leave their warm homes and confront the elements. In Council Bluffs, a flame from the fire was preserved in anticipation of the following summer when commemorative wagon trains would arrive there for the Grand Encampment celebration.

A bonfire provides scant heat for those awaiting Nauvoo commemorative program in February. Many Iowa communities lit similar fires in memory of the pioneer hardships.

9

Lined up facing the frigid Mississippi River, a group of wagons represents the hasty flight from Nauvoo. Mobs didn't allow early Saints to await better weather.

SCENE FROM THE PAST: HORSES AND WAGONS ON THE MISSISSIPPI

Call it a symbolic representation or simply a news media photo opportunity, but it constituted a dramatic beginning to the great Mormon trek re-enactment of 1996-97.

On June 17, 1996, some 15 wagons and 35 horses crossed the Mississippi River on a flatboat from Nauvoo, Ill., to Montrose, Iowa. The barge made two trips with horses and wagons and a third for support vehicles, all of which were components of the JL2 Inc. Authentic Mormon Trail Wagon Train.

It was one of two commemorative wagon trains that traversed the Iowa portion of the Mormon Trail in 1996. Participants in the Iowa Mormon Trails Association wagon train crossed the river

Wagons take a ride themselves, en route to the western shore of the Mississippi where they then became the mode of transportation for the trek across Iowa.

via a bridge at nearby Keokuk, Iowa, then camped for a week near Montrose for the start of their journey.

The river crossing at Nauvoo took some careful planning, according to William D. Price, an LDS public affairs missionary who helped coordinate the sesquicentennial observance.

One of the main concerns was keeping the horses from being spooked as they floated on the water. This was accomplished by loading the wagons around the perimeter of the barge and putting down hay between

Horses were placed in deep straw at the center of the flatboat to keep them from being uneasy on the river crossing.

them 18-24 inches deep for the horses. Planks leading onto the barge were placed solidly so the horses would not perceive them as a cattle guard. Each horseman led his animal onto the boat and stayed with it the entire way across the river. In this manner, the crossing was made without mishap.

The barge just happened to be available when it was needed. Earlier in the year it was carrying vehicle traffic across the river near Hannibal, Mo. It would have been ferrying grain any later. Operators agreed to provide the barge for the Nauvoo re-enactment for the cost of fuel, less than $200.

Preparing the site for the crossing was a challenge. The ferry landing at the end of Parley Street, where the 1846 pioneers crossed the river, today is partially under water due to a dam at Keokuk. Over the years, the city streets department had dumped concrete and steel debris at the river bank near the foot of the street. That had to be removed and replaced with clean fill for the boat crossing. As an Iowan and a non-Mormon, wagon-train organizer Leon Wilkinson used his influence with the City Council to accomplish that.

Elder and Sister Kenneth Walden are silhouetted against the western sky, symbolizing the spirit of pioneering, then and now.

I *hope that we shall never, in all the history of this church, ever forget those who came this way 150 years ago.*

President Gordon B. Hinckley,
The Church of Jesus Christ of Latter-day Saints.

11

Another obstacle was the depth of the river. The barge needed about 6 feet of water 12 feet out, and measurements revealed there simply was not that much depth. Organizers got the dam operators to bypass the red tape that would have been required and simply let more water accumulate behind the dam, allowing for the clearance needed by the barge.

Thus, events and small miracles converged to allow horses and wagons to be ferried across the Mississippi from Nauvoo for the first time in 150 years.

Ready to begin the 1996 commemorative journey across the Mississippi into Iowa, wagons assembled in Nauvoo in mid-June.

Modern pioneers tug a covered wagon down Nauvoo's Parley Street to load it onto the flatboat. Interested local residents, church members and participants lined the street to watch.

Circled in a grassy pasture in Nauvoo in the summer of 1996, wagons wait the call to begin the re-enactment journey. The expulsion from Nauvoo in the winter of 1846 was the start of a migration without equal in American history.

I O W A :

O N   T O   T H E   G R A N D   E N C A M P M E N T

To say that Iowans energetically supported the Mormon Trail sesquicentennial in 1996-97 is an understatement. They assumed a proprietary interest in it.

Iowa became a state on Dec. 28, 1846, and observance of the Mormon trek anniversary was a central part of its own statehood sesquicentennial celebration in 1996. Iowa's 1846 territorial census of 102,388 people included more than 13,000 Mormons on their way west.

The Iowa Mormon Trails Association was founded a few years before the sesquicentennial. It includes members such as Paul and Karla Gunzenhauser at Garden Grove and Bob and Beverly Brown at Mount Pisgah — who have used bent coat-hanger wires as divining rods to find traces of Mormon settlements and encampments on their land — and D. Elbert Pidcock of Corydon, who diligently researched the site where "Come, Come, Ye Saints" was written.

A commemorative wagon train was the centerpiece of the Iowa association's Mormon Trail observance. It left Nauvoo on June 17, 1996, and arrived at Council Bluffs July 12, 1996, following the main route traversed by Brigham Young's Camp of Israel group from March 1 through June 13, 1846. But it also celebrated the journeys of all the Latter-day Saints who made their way across Iowa Territory at various times and following various routes in 1846, some living there for as long as six years before joining the rest of the Saints in the Salt Lake Valley.

Nearly every town and hamlet along the way welcomed the IMTA wagon train and/or the smaller JL2 Inc. train with some sort of celebration.

In 1997, the two wagon trains formed the nucleus of the venture that followed the trail the rest of the way, crossing Nebraska and Wyoming and reaching Salt Lake City on July 22, 1997.

IOWA WAS THE CRUCIBLE WHERE THE SAINTS BECAME PIONEERS

The westward trek of Brigham Young and his followers is widely remembered as an 1847 event, yet for much of the drama, one must look to the previous year, when the Saints made their way across the muddy flats and rolling hills of southern Iowa.

William Clayton's writing of "Come, Come, Ye Saints;" establishment of semipermanent settlements at Kanesville, Garden Grove and Mt. Pisgah; the enlistment of the Mormon Battalion; the suffering of the poor camps relieved by the miracle of the quail, all occurred in Iowa in 1846, the year the territory was admitted to the union as a state.

Contrary to popular imagination, the Nauvoo exiles did not move out all at once. Rather, most left in small groups over the course of months as preparations could be made. An attempt in January to organize the exodus with captains over hundreds, fifties and tens disintegrated in the urgency to escape mob persecution.

The Camp of Israel, led by Brigham Young and members of the Quorum of the Twelve, took 131 days to traverse the 300 miles of Iowa prairie in cold, wet weather, their wagons often in axle-deep mud, before settling at Kanesville, now Council Bluffs. But the bulk of the Saints left in the spring, and many were strung out across Iowa in some 70 provisional settlements between the Mississippi River on the east and the Missouri on the west. The largest of these were Garden Grove and Mt. Pisgah, established by church leaders as way stations for those to follow.

Garden Grove was founded April 23 on 300 fertile acres with abundant timber. A town by that name exists today and has named its school district, elementary school and junior-senior high school after the Mormon Trail.

On May 12, apostle Parley P. Pratt scouted out a tract with grassy, sloping hills. In his delight he named it Mt. Pisgah after the location from which Moses saw the promised land (Deut. 3:27.) As many as 2,000 Saints lived there. A monument stands there today marking a burial ground. It was placed by the LDS Church in 1888 and inscribed with 64 names of people who died at Mt. Pisgah.

The events of the 1846 Iowa crossing were collectively commemorated in the summer of 1996 by two wagon trains that departed from Nauvoo June 17.

The Iowa Mormon Trails Association, with chapters in the trail's 12 counties, set out with 18 wagons, though 60 were enrolled and participated along the trail before its arrival at Council Bluffs on July 12 for the Grand Encampment celebration.

A private company, JL2 Inc., set out with 13 wagons and arrived with eight at Omaha, Neb., on July 4, where it participated in a parade at historic Winter Quarters.

Along the way, townspeople spruced up homes and barns and turned out to welcome the wagon trains at dozens of festivals and celebrations,

giving water to trekkers and offering to move their support vehicles for them. Among highlights:

• The IMTA train camped for a week at Montrose, Iowa, across the river from Nauvoo. Participants remembered that it was near Montrose on October 9, 1846, where the final group of Saints evacuating Nauvoo was rescued from starvation as a flock of exhausted quail descended on

*A modern family plays pioneer to commemorate
the trials of handcart companies
that made the trek west in the mid-1850s.*

*Wagon wheels draw squiggly trails on a muddy Iowa road. The hardships
of the Iowa crossing in 1846 prepared the migrating Saints for the longer pull
to the Great Basin in the Rocky Mountains the following year.*

17

Pro football star Steve Young, a great-great-great-grandson of Brigham Young, portrays his famous pioneer ancestor during ceremony in Council Bluffs, Iowa, re-enacting the mustering in of the Mormon Battalion.

their camp. It was a remarkable replay of the miracle that saved Moses' Israelites as they were wandering in the wilderness.

• Near Murray, Iowa, they camped in wagon wheel ruts made 150 years earlier by the original pioneers.

• At the Van Buren County Courthouse in Keosauqua on June 25, wagon-train participants were present as a re-creation of William Pitt's brass band repeated history. Directed by J. Mark Ammons of Culver-Stockton College in Missouri, it performed in the same courtroom where the original band gave a concert on June 25, 1846. While crossing Iowa, the original Pitt's band performed for Iowa residents and earned much-needed cash to buy provisions for the pioneers' trek.

In 1997, the two wagon trains were consolidated in the single train that continued the rest of the way to Salt Lake City, crossing Nebraska and Wyoming and into northern Utah.

Wagon train traverses rolling hills of southwest Iowa between Macedonia and Council Bluffs as part of the 150th anniversary celebration of the Mormon Trail.

COME, COME, YE SAINTS

William Clayton was in a jubilant mood when he wrote "Come, Come, Ye Saints" on April 15, 1846. As clerk of Brigham Young's "Camp of Israel," Clayton shouldered much official responsibility in addition to the burden of caring for three wives, five children and his mother on the trek. Moreover, he was worried about his 17-year-old fourth wife, Diantha, whom he had left in Nauvoo because she was pregnant and unable to travel. Then came the news, secondhand via a letter to a camp member: Diantha had given birth to a son, a "fine, fat boy," on March 30.

"Truly I feel to rejoice at this intelligence," he wrote, then added, "This morning I composed a new song — 'All Is Well.' "

With words set to a popular English melody of the day, the new song caught on immediately. It became the anthem of the entire Mormon pioneer epoch and is perhaps the song most closely associated with the LDS Church today. It bespeaks optimism and assurance that ultimate joy awaits those who faithfully endure adversity.

Working from state historical documents, survey maps and courthouse records, Wayne County, Iowa, historian D. Elbert Pidcock pinpointed the campsite at Locust Creek where Clayton wrote his famous hymn. Based on his research, the LDS Church and the county historical society in 1990 placed a marker near there, at the entrance to Tharp Cemetery. (The cemetery bears no relationship to Mormon history; it is merely a convenient place for the marker.)

On Feb. 4, 1996, at the behest of *Des Moines Register* columnist Chuck Offenburger, churches of various denominations throughout Iowa sang "Come, Come, Ye Saints" in consideration of that day's

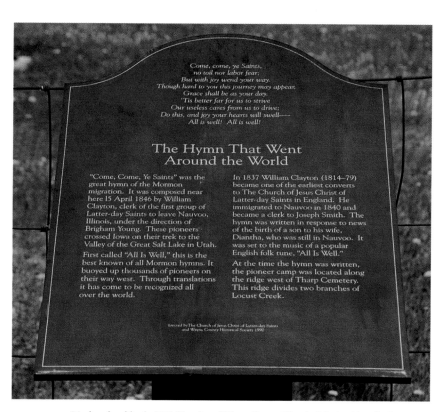

Marker placed by the LDS Church and Wayne County Historical Society identifies location on Mormon Trail near Seymour, Iowa, where William Clayton wrote "Come, Come, Ye Saints."

commemoration of the sesquicentennial of the Nauvoo exodus.

On April 14 of that year, Corydon, Iowa, observed "Come, Come, Ye Saints" Day. The town museum has a permanent exhibit commemorating "the hymn that went around the world."

And on July 1, the Iowa Mormon Trails Association wagon train camped and about 1,000 people gathered at Locust Creek Camp No. 2 to remember the writing of the hymn on that spot. The previous evening, in nearby Seymour, a 150-voice community choir sang the hymn at a program in the high school gymnasium.

THE GRAND ENCAMPMENT RAISES
MEMORIES OF SOLDIERS AND A HYMN

The re-enactment of the Mormon pioneer trek across the rolling hills of Iowa during the summer of 1996 ended with a Grand Encampment Celebration in Council Bluffs, Iowa.

A number of wagons and several handcarts pulled onto the campus of the Iowa School for the Deaf July 12, amid the cheers and applause of hundreds of well-wishers and curious onlookers carrying cameras and camcorders to record the arrival of the modern-day pioneers. The travelers made the 300-mile trek across 13 southern Iowa counties in 3 1/2 weeks. They were commemorating the 150th anniversary of the 1846 exodus of the Mormons from Nauvoo.

Re-enacting the Iowa portion of the Mormon pioneer trail trek was a precursor to the much longer and more difficult 1997 re-enactment through Nebraska, Wyoming and Utah.

The two days of celebration in Council Bluffs took its name from the huge pioneer encampment on the eastern banks of the Missouri River in 1846. Within a month after the first pioneers arrived there on June 14, 1846, as many as 10,000 Mormon refugees reached the encampment. By the fall of 1846, that number swelled to 13,000. The vast collection of people, livestock, wagons and tents became known as the Grand Encampment and stretched back to the east for nine miles.

The original encampment began on the site where the 140-year-old school for the deaf is located today. There on its campus, the commemorative celebration of the sesquicentennial of the

During dedicatory ceremony of reconstructed Kanesville tabernacle, young people peer through window to catch a glimpse of what's going on inside.

Speaking in reconstructed Kanesville log tabernacle, President Gordon B. Hinckley addresses audience as interpreter provides sign language. Brigham Young was sustained as LDS Church president in original tabernacle in 1847.

Mormon Trail, as well as the 150th anniversary of Iowa statehood and of the founding of Council Bluffs, was held.

"This is historic ground," said President Gordon B. Hinckley of The Church of Jesus Christ of Latter-day Saints. He addressed some 12,500 people at an outdoor devotional on the evening of July 13. "This is hallowed ground. This is ground where our forebears lived for a season."

President Hinckley told of the conditions under which William Clayton, on the trail in Iowa, wrote the words of "Come, Come, Ye Saints" and recited some of the lyrics.

That hymn, President Hinckley said, "became the theme song of our people crossing the Plains, of the tens of thousands who moved through here, this place of grand encampment, this very soil on which you sit this evening.

"It was a remarkable thing, the movement of our people from Nauvoo and its environs to the valleys of the West. This was a place for rest and the fitting out for the long journey that lay ahead," President Hinckley told the large audience that packed the grounds, many of whom were dressed in clothing fashioned after the pioneer era.

Earlier in the day, President Hinckley dedicated the reconstructed Kanesville Tabernacle, a replica of the old log tabernacle where Brigham Young was sustained as second president of the church in December 1847. The original tabernacle, measuring 40 feet by 60 feet and said to be the

Horse-drawn wagon pulls up in front of reconstructed Kanesville tabernacle, bringing dignitaries to dedicatory ceremony and adding a touch of realism to the setting.

21

largest log cabin in the world, was built because there was no facility large enough to hold all the people who wanted to attend a church conference there. It was at that conference where the just-reorganized First Presidency was sustained by the general membership.

About 400 invited guests attended the dedicatory services of the newly built tabernacle, located in downtown Council Bluffs, which was once known as Kanesville. Kanesville today remains a name with a lasting place in LDS Church history, a name second only to Winter Quarters in historical prominence and name recognition from the Iowa-Nebraska period.

Steve Young, star quarterback for the San Francisco 49ers and a great-great-great-grandson of Brigham Young, spoke at both the Grand Encampment devotional and at the tabernacle dedication.

The Grand Encampment also included a re-enactment of the mustering-in of the Mormon Battalion and a dance patterned after a cotillion held the night before the battalion marched off for military service.

After the events of the two-day encampment came to a close, wagon train and handcart participants returned to their homes. Many would join the commemorative wagon train the next year for the long and arduous trek into the Salt Lake Valley.

22

Above, President Gordon B. Hinckley addresses a large crowd at Council Bluffs gathering. Programs and events focused on the Grand Encampment of 1846 and the mustering of the Mormon Battalion the same year. Right, young square dancers memorialize the cotillion that allowed Battalion members of 150 years ago to enjoy a last evening with their families.

A NEW GENERATION ENLISTS IN THE MORMON BATTALION

Brigham Young's promise that the Mormon Battalion members would be held "in honorable remembrance" came true in the sesquicentennial observances of 1996-97.

In June 1846, U.S. President James K. Polk ordered the enlistment of 500 westward-bound Mormons in the war with Mexico. The directive must have seemed highly audacious to most of the Nauvoo exiles, then in the act of leaving the United States borders to escape religious persecution to which the federal government had acquiesced.

What they soon came to understand, however, was that President Young not only approved of the call for enlistees, he in fact helped orchestrate it. Acting as his agent, Eastern States Mission President Jesse C. Little met with Polk and facilitated the call.

Col. Thomas L. Kane, who would be a friend and benefactor to the LDS people, carried Polk's orders to Col. Stephen W. Kearny at Fort Leavenworth, Kan., who in turn issued an order to Captain James Allen of the First Dragoons.

With the aid of President Young, Allen enlisted 520 men over a three-week period. They were mustered

Above, Jean duVal Kane, a descendant of Thomas L. Kane, great friend and defender of the Saints, attended the Council Bluffs events. Right, Members of the North American Central Area Choir put feeling into a rendition of "Battle Hymn of the Republic."

into service at Kanesville on July 16, and with 35 women, including laundresses, and 42 children, including servants to officers, went to Fort Leavenworth, where they were outfitted and received their orders. Their march of over 2,000 miles took them to San Diego, Calif., via Santa Fe, N.M. They served in garrison duty at San Diego, Mission San Luis Rey and Los Angeles. Working for John Sutter after their discharge, some former battalion soldiers played a part in the discovery of gold at Sacramento.

I'll always remember the incredible spirit felt along the trail. I have great admiration for all the original pioneers.

Mindy Pitcher, Alpine, Utah

23

Marching to the drummer's beat, members of the newly mustered Mormon Battalion pass in review. This scene was re-enacted to remember the 150th anniversary of the mustering in of the battalion.

In accordance with Brigham Young's strategy, the battalion's enlistment brought advantages to the Latter-day Saints' cause: The soldiers' army pay and uniform allowance gave financial support to the pioneers. The enlistment demonstrated the loyalty of the Mormon people to the United States. It brought a portion of them west at government expense. And their pioneering efforts established routes from the Rocky Mountains to the coast.

Remembrance of the battalion was virtually a celebration within a celebration during the 1996-97 Pioneer Sesquicentennial. The Grand Encampment festivities at Council Bluffs, Iowa, July 13, 1996, included a re-enactment of the historic mustering-in ceremony of 1846. Witnessed by a crowd of 9,500 at the campus of the Iowa School for the Deaf, it featured a march by five companies of battalion descendants dressed in period clothing.

Other battalion commemorations followed. At Fort Leavenworth on Aug. 3, 1996, costumed re-enactors from six LDS stakes in Kansas and Missouri marched a half-mile to the parade ground. They and spectators heard speeches from LDS leaders and a brigadier-general at the post.

Drummer Ryan Curtis of Greendale, Wis., leads Company A. During the re-enactment five companies, composed of descendants of original battalion members, marched in review.

Above, Garn Hatch, a member of the present-day commemorative Mormon Battalion, was an enthusiastic participant in the Council Bluffs re-enactment. Right, hand raised to the square, a volunteer re-enacting the mustering of the Mormon Battalion represents historic Battalion member Jefferson Hunt.

25

NEBRASKA:
SAND HILLS & FLAT LANDS

Months of preparation were over. Gathered in Omaha, Nebraska's Miller Park, a group of several hundred fresh and eager pioneers heard farewell speeches from church and government dignitaries, then hit the trail on April 21, 1997. Ahead were Nebraska's gentle hills, rolling away from the Missouri River toward the prairie flatlands to the west.

By the time central Nebraska's sandhills were sucking at their wagon wheels, the camp had largely settled into a routine. Blisters, balky animals, early-trip logistic snafus, long weary days, relatively primitive amenities, lumpy roads and an unpredictable succession of too-wet rain and too-hot sun had become realities.

For most of the modern pioneers, hardships were balanced by blossoming friendships, spiritual renewal, the longed-for sense of kinship with the past and the daily adventure of the trail. Enthusiasm was constantly rekindled with the arrival of short-term trekkers eager to share in the experience. Landmarks such as Chimney Rock and Scottsbluff presaged the Wyoming border and the trek's halfway mark.

THE FIRST ASSAULT BEGINS ON A 1,100 MILE JOURNEY

With a light mist frosting the Missouri River and the sun barely topping poplars that line the prairie horizon, several dozen upbeat "pioneers" left Council Bluffs, Iowa, April 19, 1997, and headed west.

They were the vanguard of thousands of marchers who would trek part or all of the 1,100-mile Mormon Trail to Salt Lake City during the summer of 1997. They planned to re-enact the historic Latter-day Saint migration that began in April 1847. Their trek would also be historic — perhaps the last one possible on the old Mormon Trail.

The small group, riding in light wagons, on horseback or ambling on foot down a dusty country road, followed the Oxbow Trail, a route slightly south of that taken by most of the pioneers in the period from 1847 to 1869.

Meanwhile, a much larger group assembled in north Omaha, Neb., to depart April 21 along the northern trail. The two groups later united near Kearney, Neb., and continued the journey together.

The dedication of a visitors center in historic Winter Quarters, (now in north Omaha's Florence district), where the early Latter-day Saints spent a miserable winter preparing for their mass journey west, set a tone for the re-enactment.

President Gordon B. Hinckley of The Church of Jesus Christ of Latter-day Saints flew over more of the United States in one day than his predecessor, Brigham Young, covered in three months. President Hinckley dedicated the center at the foot of Cemetery Hill. The poignant graves of several hundred would-be pioneers who never lived to make the trek reminded a large audience of the heavy sacrifices made to re-settle the Latter-day Saints in a new Zion.

A long haul up a muddy hill challenges handcart crews and walkers during the first week in Nebraska. Rain accompanied the train out of Omaha and kept it company for several days.

28

President Gordon B. Hinckley dedicated a new visitors center at the historic Winter Quarters site before bidding the wagon train goodbye.

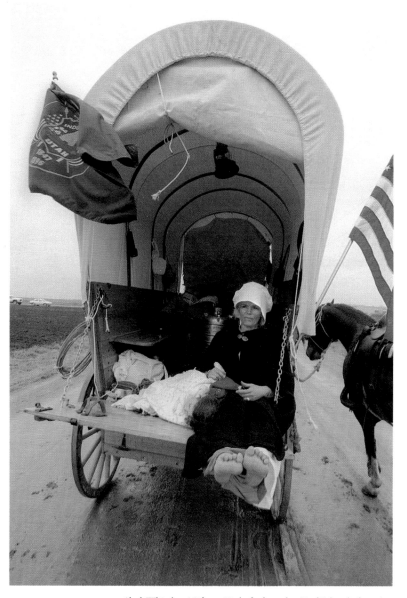

Although the early Saints found temporary respite from their flight at Winter Quarters, President Hinckley said, "This was not the right place. I am grateful our people didn't stop here. It was not far enough to escape their persecutions." History has since proved that pioneer leader Brigham Young was correct in declaring the then-isolated Great Salt Lake Valley "the place," he said.

"They were great people in whose footsteps we walk. They did what they set out to do."

President Hinckley exchanged gifts with Nebraska Gov. E. Benjamin Nelson. Nelson spoke of the shared history of the Latter-day Saints and his state and said that seeing the Great Salt Lake earlier gave him a sense of the magnitude of the task undertaken by the pioneers of the 1800s.

After a Sabbath Day rest, President Hinckley and other church and government leaders again spoke to the modern trekkers as they waited under fog-shrouded trees in Miller Park for the signal to begin their adventure.

"We look forward to meeting you when you complete the journey," he said. "We will be there (in Salt Lake City) to say hello as we are here to say goodbye. May God be with you, may his watchful care be over you, may you be happy as you re-enact one of the great movements of all time."

Nebraska wagonmaster Joe Vogel, riding tall in the saddle, was busy lining up wagons, handcarts and walkers for their exit from the park. But the 1997 pioneers had some problems their earlier counterparts

Aleah Whitaker, Midway, Utah, finds mother Linda's lap the best place for a snooze during an exhausting day early in the trek.

29

The cover of a handcart, above left, echoes sentiment often expressed by those who pushed and pulled: There are angels among us. Below left, Margaret Rowland, Spanish Fork, Utah, was typical. She had vintage clothing and a modern camera as she waited the arrival of President Hinckley for farewell ceremony in Omaha, Neb. Above, a wagon and team is limned by a setting sun somewhere in Nebraska.

30

would have been astounded to witness. The train was held up for several minutes to await the arrival of local police officers. They blocked traffic temporarily on Omaha's busy 30th Street so modern and vintage vehicles would not collide.

Once on the move, however, the line of wagons, followed by its horse and human entourage, made its first assault on the 1,100 miles that lay ahead.

Draft animals got their first taste of the uphill parts of the trail as they clopped up the steep grade of State Street, past the church's new visitors center and the pioneer cemetery and on to the farm-dotted landscape outside Omaha.

Many of those who thought they would stay the course clear to Salt Lake City would drop out, Vogel predicted. But for Day One, at least, it was "wagons, ho!" with enthusiasm.

31

Strung out over a mile of Nebraska country road, the wagon train advances though verdant farmland green from spring rains, with wagonmaster Joe Vogel at its head.

32

EMOTIONAL MOMENTS HONOR THE TRAIL'S YOUNGEST VICTIMS

Of the 6,000 who died among the original Latter-day Saint pioneers, many were infants or small children too fragile to withstand the demands of the long trail to Zion.

For those making the 1997 trek, nothing brought the sacrifice of the early pioneers so sharply into focus as the graves of children whose small remains were left in haste at trailside.

At two Nebraska sites, the short lives of such children were memorialized as symbolic of the many who died.

For little John McBride Belnap, the Mormon Trail ended almost as it began. The 13-month old son of Gilbert and Adaline Knight Belnap contracted cholera, a common killer among the emigrants, during a camp epidemic. He quickly died near the Salt River at what ultimately became Ashland, Neb.

The second little one whose grave called for tender reflection by the modern trekkers left no name. Only a small stone marks the spot that people in Sutherland, Neb., have held in respect for years without knowing the details of the baby's life. Local lore holds that the grave is that of a 2- or 3-month old boy whose parents buried him, then continued on their journey to the West.

At Ashland, located on the Oxbow, or southern, Mormon Trail, members of the Belnap Family Association, now thousands in number, took advantage of the wagon train re-enactment to dedicate a marker to John McBride. Wagon train members and community residents joined in the event. The five-foot marker of gray Utah marble stands near the site indicated in early family writings as the grave.

Wendy Westergard, Salt Lake City, left, and Christina Dicken, Plymouth, Wash., share a tender moment during the rededication of a small grave near Sutherland.

Les Hill, Sugar City, Idaho, current president of the family organization, dedicated the marker.

When the baby died, there was no wood available for a coffin. The grieving Gilbert Belnap tenderly wrapped his son's remains in a quilt and placed the body in his tool box for burial.

As part of the memorial, the family commissioned the construction of a tool box as nearly the same as possible to the burial box. Artifacts, including aged copies of LDS Scriptures, vintage tools and a baby blanket and shoes, were placed in the box.

The box was carted from Council Bluffs, Iowa, to Ashland, Neb., in the wagon of Ray and Pat Hailey, LDS Church members from New Virginia, Iowa. After the ceremony, the tool box went back into the Hailey's wagon for the duration of the trip to Utah. It will become a family "time capsule" for the Belnaps, to be reopened in 2097 as a tangible reminder of the family's pioneer heritage.

In Sutherland, wagon train participants joined with community history buffs and officials on May 20 to rededicate the grave of the unknown baby whose death is memorialized only by a plain unmarked stone. Children from the wagon train respectfully decorated the grave with weeds and wildflowers, and wagon train President Brian Hill, also president of Kearney Nebraska Stake, tearfully dedicated the small plot as a symbol of the many children whose trip to Zion ended far too short of the goal.

The replica of an old tool chest in which baby John McBride Belnap was buried near Ashland, Neb., was precious cargo for Pat and Ray Hailey of Iowa.

Children of the 1997 wagon train used prairie weeds to decorate the slab of stone marking the grave of an unknown little pioneer near Sutherland.

DEEP SAND STILL PULLS ON TODAY'S WAGON WHEELS

Ages ago, glaciers scoured the American midlands. The Platte River, young, much larger and more rambunctious than now, rampaged through what was to become Nebraska. Together, they piled up 10,000 square miles of sand dunes that challenged the Latter-day Saint pioneers of the mid-1800s — and those following on the trail in the summer of 1997.

After keeping close to the shores of the Platte River for some time, the 1847 pioneers finally had to move into the sand hills because of steep bluffs that came right to the river's side. It was a test for man and beast as wagons and walkers bogged in the deep sand.

The 1997 caravan, with more than 300 miles of the 1,100-mile journey behind, marched into the sand hills near Hershey, Neb., on May 20. The modern train had followed primarily developed roads to this point, but it digressed briefly for a demonstration of what the sand hills were like for the earlier pioneers.

A group of representative wagons slogged through a portion of the hills to get the feel of sand pulling at the wheels. For chosen handcart crews, it was also sand pulling at their heels as they took a step forward and a slide back on the shifty ground. After a half day in the mushy soil, the handcart gangs and walkers were ready to collapse onto any bit of shade they could find for a few minutes of recuperation.

For part of the distance over the sand hills, the wagons followed the eroded ruts of the earlier migration. Wheels cut so deeply into the prairie sand 150 years ago that the ruts have never been fully covered by the bunch grass and blue stem that top the rest of the land.

A guest in the lead wagon was Gary Trego, whose family owns the property the wagon train crossed this day. He said that the sand hills had less plant cover when Brigham Young led the vanguard group through here in 1847. Modern farmers and ranchers work at preserving the ground cover,

A group of representative wagons pushes through the mushy terrain of Nebraska's sandhills near Hershey. Ruts created by wagon trains in the 1800s still scar the area.

Helping hands strain to right the Wyoming state wagon after it teetered and fell in a sandy path through the Nebraska sandhills. Four riders were uninjured.

Ethan Lowe, 2, of Spanish Fork, Utah, lifts a tent flap to watch the goings-on in Omaha, Neb. Such flimsy quarters would be home for the next three months.

and that is the best protection the historic ruts can have as well, he said.

There was a moment of pioneer reality in the 1997 re-creation as the second wagon in the demonstration group — Wyoming's official vehicle — started down a sand hill and began to teeter on the uneven terrain. After righting itself a couple of times, the wagon went into an irreversible tilt and landed softly on its right side.

"Now, that's something for my journal," said Salt Laker Sandy Van Leeuwen. She and her husband, Tom, were passengers in the wagon driven by Wyoming wagonmaster Ben Kern. The Van Leeuwens and another passenger, Candy Moulton, were uninjured in the tipover, and the mules pulling the vehicle remained standing.

The minor accident was a harbinger. The following day, as the train took off onto a barely marked prairie trail, horseback rider Walter Okamoto of West Point, Utah, wheeled his horse to change direction and the animal stepped into a hole, throwing Okamoto off and rolling over him.

Prairie ingenuity took over as one wagon driver found a piece of wood strong enough to hold the injured man, and a television crewman offered a roll of gaffer tape to complete a makeshift stretcher. A local doctor determined that Okamoto's leg was not broken, and he was treated and released. A few days later he was back on the trail.

A short time after Okamoto's spill, a horse named April balked at pulling a buggy through the deep sand. She picked a poor place to rebel, slipped off the edge of a rut and ended up on her side, taking the buggy over with her. Horsemen responded quickly, bent the buggy shafts straight and helped Mervin Bennion of West Jordan, Utah get on the road again.

At the morning meeting, chief camp jack Bob Haderle had warned of "creepy crawlies. Be very, very careful. We're getting into an area where you'll have to watch for snakes. Don't mess with them. The last thing we want to do is treat someone for snakebite."

Timewise, a third of the way now lay behind the trekkers, and everything was "going absolutely perfect," said Nebraska wagonmaster Joe Vogel, who had given a month's worth of "wagon hos" each morning.

A worn-out boot slipped over a fence post keeps silent vigil over the Nebraska landscape as the wagon train files past — an omen, perhaps, of the wear and tear on thousands of shoes treading the trail.

ON A PERSONAL NOTE, A CHANCE TO WALK WHERE ANCESTORS TROD

By Twila Van Leer

So this is how they came. All those pioneer ancestors whose names decorate my family tree: the Pecks, the Matthewses, the Van Ordens, the Haights, the Taylors, the Gagons and many more.

I was pleased with my assignment to report on the sesquicentennial re-enactment of the crossing of the plains. I would get to taste, if possible, the experience of those progenitors.

How authentic was the experience? Total authenticity is impossible 150 years after the fact. Most of the trail has long since disappeared under farmland, towns and the highways that whistle today's travelers along the route in jig time.

But the feel of the trek is there for those with a little imagination. The eastern Nebraska terrain still undulates gradually onto more level ground. And weather remains no respecter of people or projects.

Perched on the seat of Nebraska's official wagon, I could appreciate the feelings of those first pioneers. With the Omaha skyline fast disappearing, I could sense what it felt like then, leaving behind what was familiar and venturing into Indian territory.

The bustle of the first-morning camp breaking up was real enough. In a drizzling rain, dawn was apparent only by a change from dark gray to a lighter gray. Youngsters who had danced in the stubble to fiddle music the night before huddled into their plastic ponchos and waited to be on their way.

Wagonmaster Joe Vogel hustled to organize — wagons first, handcarts in the middle, walkers in the rear. One by one the wagons pulled out of

Ryan Whitaker, Midway, Utah, rides away from a windmill after watering his horse prior to another day's march through Nebraska's sandhills.

37

For handcart push-pull crews, the sandy crust of central Nebraska was a particular challenge.
A step forward and a slide back was standard progress.

the night's circle, jolted down the slope of a farm field, across the barrow and onto the muddy country road. Within a half hour, the train was strung out a mile.

Dolly and Babe, a pair of patient gray Percherons, plodded through the beautiful Nebraska farmland, heads down against the rain. Here, contour plowing creates an artwork in nature, broken by handsome clusters of farm buildings, fences and stands of trees that were not yet saplings when my forebears passed by.

When we took off, the rain was exciting atmosphere. It became a miserable reality as the day wore on. A perpetual stream dripped off the nose of our teamster, sitting out in the elements. I soon felt damp through several layers of clothing. For my ancestors, "wet" must have been a constant until the weather changed — to be replaced, no doubt, by "hot" or "wind" or even "snow."

I'll bet my great-grandmothers had the same hopes for a change in topography that would offer easier travel, only to find that each hilltop revealed another hill looming ahead. When we rolled effortlessly over several streams flowing under culverts, I could imagine what an obstacle they could be if I had to jump from the wagon and help dig down the banks to make a wagon path or — perish the thought — ferry myself and goods across wider streams.

By nightfall, the trekkers were camped in a muddy field next to a busy highway. The rain continued to fall, and I marveled that disgruntlement had not set in. These modern pioneers are made of the same sturdy goods as those who made the trip in the 1800s.

Authentic? No, but a little taste was enough to increase my appreciation for my pioneer kin. Pray that fortitude, courage, faith and commitment are passed through the genes to our new generations as we follow trails that are different but just as challenging.

Shawn Merrill, Orem, Utah, found cleaning his boots in Nebraska just as distasteful as cleaning them back home.

On the trail, home is where you hang your tophat — or sunbonnet.

39

Grant, Josh, Christian and Russell Peterson, Blue Springs, Mo., whoop it up, upper left, already on an imaginary trail before the wagons take off. Right, school children in Omaha, Neb. exchange howdies with a teamster and below, handcarts pass through the stubble of last year's corn crop early in the trek.

40

'Wow! Now that's a lot of horsepower!' might be the thought passing through the mind of 2-year-old
Ethan Lowe, Spanish Fork, Utah, who is dwarfed by the draft animals.

PART FOUR

WYOMING:
OVER THE DIVIDE

On May 31, 1847, Brigham Young and his pioneer band entered what, 43 long years later, would be declared the state of Wyoming. The Nebraska prairies were giving way to hillier country, harbinger of the mountains to come.

The sesquicentennial trekkers, crossing the boundary where no boundary used to exist, found the state's mountain-ringed prairies lush from spring rains. The wagon train traded travel on private lands for public lands through much of the state, sometimes rolling on paved roads that were more difficult for animals and foot trekkers than the dirt byways.

A 31-mile march broke the trek record for distance in a day. Stops at Fort Laramie, Fort Caspar, Independence Rock, Martin's Cove, Simpsons Hollow, the Lombard ferry site on the Green River and Fort Bridger strengthened ties to a past when these sites were milestones in LDS history.

Angling southwest, the terrain began to change. Mesas and low hills were replaced on the horizon by snow-capped mountains. In the least-densely populated state in the West, crowds still assembled to meet and mingle with the wagon train participants, and local newspapers from Laramie to Evanston made it the story of the day.

INDEPENDENCE ROCK — A MILESTONE IN BOTH AGES

Programs on both sides of the Nebraska/Wyoming state line in early June marked a significant milestone for the trekkers of the Mormon Trail Wagon Train re-enactment.

In the tiny hamlet of Henry, Neb., on June 3, E. Benjamin Nelson of Nebraska passed the role of host governor to Jim Geringer of Wyoming. The next night, in Torrington, a short way into Wyoming, Nebraska wagonmaster Joe Vogel "passed the reins" to Wyoming wagonmaster Ben Kern, and the train marched on with approximately half of the journey behind.

From June 13-15, President Thomas S. Monson, first counselor in the First Presidency of The Church of Jesus Christ of Latter-day Saints, met with the trekkers to offer encouragement and visit some of the pioneer sites that mark Wyoming's northeast corner.

In an outdoor fireside June 15 at Fort Caspar, with a big tent protecting a mingled crowd of trekkers and local residents from atypically heavy rain, President Monson congratulated the travelers for persevering like true pioneers.

President Thomas S. Monson had a handshake for young pioneer fans at Fort Caspar as the train took Wyoming in stride.

"You've got the horses, you've got the mules, you've got the leather on your shoes, the spirit in your heart and the nobility of soul and you're on the way to the valley of the

The bumpy terrain of Rocky Ridge was a challenge for the 1800s pioneers — and for some of those of the commemorative wagon train.

Early pioneer Milo J. Ayer dug deep into Independence rock so modern trekkers could easily spot his signature.

Shauna Dicken, Plymouth, Wash., had to wade a marsh to get to the signature — worn into near-illegibility — of her ancestor, P.G. Sessions.

mountains," he said. "Many of you are members of the Mormon faith; others aren't, but you're having a great time together."

Earlier, he and his wife, Frances, visited Rocky Ridge, at 7,300 feet the highest point traversed along the trail, short of the Wasatch range, and Rock Creek and Martin's Cove. It was at these last two sites that the Willie and Martin handcart companies suffered terribly in winter storms of 1856, leaving 200 dead. President Monson recalled the charity of a kinsman, Gibson Condie, who participated in a rescue effort for the handcart survivors. At Martin's Cove, the church leader addressed about 2,000 LDS Boy Scouts gathered for a Jamboree.

On June 17 the train arrived at Independence Rock, one of the landmarks that earlier pioneers anticipated with eagerness.

Aaaah! Modern trekkers Sarah, Nathan and Joe Winward, with Kellin Parker, dabble their feet in pools of water atop Independence Rock, just as 1800s pioneers did.

Just like William Clayton of the 1847 first company, many of the modern trekkers climbed the 136-foot high outcrop to dangle their feet in the cool puddles of water on top.

Several eras of Western American history converge at this geologic oddity. In 1812, Robert Stuart, the originator of the Oregon Trail, visited the site. But it was William Sublette who arrived at the granite outcrop on July 4, 1830, and gave it the name of America's birthday. Later travelers on the Mormon and Oregon trails tried to time their arrivals to coincide with the July 4th observance.

The Mormon Trail re-enacters were early, but it was nevertheless a highlight to be remembered. For some of the party, Independence Rock held tangible reminders of the ancestors whose journey they were celebrating. The names of hundreds of pioneers — Latter-day Saint and otherwise — are engraved in the rock.

Shauna Dicken and four daughters, Jennifer, Emily, Christina and Sarah, had to brave hordes of mosquitoes and wade through a swampy pool at the base of Independence Rock to find the name of their ancestor, P.G. (Perrigrine) Sessions. But it was a thrilling moment for them. Sessions, who crossed the plains in 1847, was one of the founders of Bountiful, Utah. His mother, Patty Bartlett Sessions, was a midwife who delivered thousands of Utah Territory's earliest residents.

"And I love him with all my heart," said Dicken, who now lives in Plymouth, Washington. Memories of pioneer ancestors have buoyed today's trekkers, she said, delicately fingering the engraved signature, worn by time and weather and nearly illegible.

President Brian Hill of the Kearney Nebraska LDS Stake and of the LDS group in the wagon train, reported the Wyoming portion of the trail "a little more rugged, a little more lonely" and Wyoming officials a little more sticky about rules and regulations. But overall, things were going well.

Gaps are for jumping. Young people in the 1997 pioneer party still had energy for such leaps despite a long, hot day on the trail.

The 136-foot summit of Independence Rock was a perfect vantage point for observers to watch the arrival of the wagon train.

NEAR DEVIL'S GATE, A TRIBUTE TO THE HANDCART TRAGEDIES

The single greatest tragedy of the Latter-day Saint pioneer epic of the 19th century cast a somber mood over the 1997 re-enactment June 18 as it passed near Martin's Cove en route to a nearby campsite.

The train filed through a gap in the hills close to Devil's Gate, the portal used by all the pioneer companies and past a new visitors center with reverence and gratitude for the sacrifices of those earlier pioneers.

The Martin and Willie handcart companies suffered extreme hardship in central Wyoming, stalled in their trek to the Great Salt Lake Valley by early snowstorms in October 1856. Of the 576 in the Martin Company, 145 perished, many of them buried in common graves. Rescuers sent by Brigham Young from Salt Lake City saved most of the survivors, but many arrived in the valley with frozen limbs and suffering from starvation and exposure.

The story now demands the respect of modern travelers, including the re-enactment participants, who passed by a memorial marker in silence and reverence.

Handcart parties were created in the mid-1850s to help bring church members who could not afford wagons and oxen to the Utah Territory. This method of emigration was short-lived, although a number of companies made the trip without incident.

As the 1997 wagon train passed near Martin's Cove, several hundred youths and leaders from the Sandy Crescent Park Stake, enjoying a summer activity in the area, cheered it on. Special applause was directed at the handcart group, which represented to the crowd that earlier, sadder time.

A strong contingent of modern handcart enthusiasts made the entire trip from Winter Quarters to Salt Lake City, pushing and pulling all the way.

Down a narrow passage through the hills near Martin's Cove, the wagon train headed into an area rich in Latter-day Saint history.

Silhouetted against a Wyoming sunrise, Utah outrider Gordon Lowe takes a short break from his trail duties.

Along the route, those providing the foot power learned that carts are a dubious method for transporting goods. For children who bounced along in the bed of a cart, however, the ride was a rare adventure. Despite the jolts, for instance, little Kinze Atkinson, part of a Phoenix, Ariz., group on the trail, didn't miss a pull on the moist thumb she had planted in her mouth. She continued sleeping as the wagon train pulled into Cherry Creek Campground just south of Martin's Cove.

The amenities of a visitors center at the Cove are recent additions. In early May 1997, President Gordon B. Hinckley dedicated the center, formerly the ranch house of Sun Ranch. In August 1992, during the dedication of a marker commemorating the Martin Company, he prayed that access to the historic sites would be improved so that many could feel the spirit of the place.

That desire was fulfilled when the church was able to purchase access to the site, with an agreement eventually to buy all of the ranch property. Many tourists and church members, including descendants of those who suffered here, have visited the site.

A special feature of the center is a list of the 1,000-plus members of the Martin and Willie handcart companies and the Hunt-Hodgett wagon companies that traveled the trail at the same time and shared many of the hardships. On this day in June 1997, their memories were venerated by the trekkers of a new generation.

As the campers rested, they paid little attention to another historic re-enactment. Kerry Roe, Evansville, Wyo., one of a group of riders re-enacting the Pony Express route from St. Joseph, Mo., to Sacramento, Calif., rode into the Cherry Creek Camp at a run. He picked up several

49

letters from Wyoming wagonmaster Ben Kern and was on his way again in true Pony Express style.

The Express operated in Utah Territory and other Western areas from April 1860 to October 1861, then died abruptly when telegraph lines linking East and West made the service obsolete.

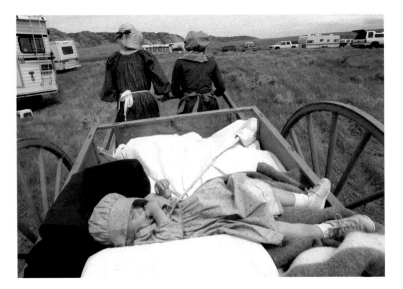

Kinze Atkinson finds the bed of a handcart perfect for napping. Those who provided the foot-power sometimes had less kindly opinions of the humble vehicle.

50

THE 'UTAH WAR' IS FOUGHT AGAIN AND A FERRY CROSSES THE GREEN

The Mormon Trail through southwestern Wyoming is rich in history, and the 1997 sesquicentennial wagon train re-enactment enjoyed heavy doses of the past while traveling through the area.

At Simpsons Hollow on July 5, the escapades of Latter-day Saint adventurer Lot Smith were commemorated. On Oct. 5, 1857, Smith and 43 members of the Utah Militia burned most of Supply Unit 10 of the Russell, Majors and Waddell supply wagon train traveling with U.S. Army troops headed for the Utah Territory. When it was over, the bullwhackers driving 25 supply wagons had given up their arms. Their leader, Lewis Simpson, also handed over his gun after a little persuasion by Smith. Twenty-three of the 25 wagons were burned, destroying valuable food and supplies that would have aided the army's cause.

The U.S. troops had been commissioned by President James Buchanan, convinced by anti-Mormon groups that a rebellion was brewing among Latter-day Saint settlers in Utah Territory. The Simpsons Hollow event and other predations by Smith's group on the federal troops probably averted a potentially devastating confrontation between the army and the settlers.

Smith's attacks were "very desperate moves on the part of a desperate people," said LDS Church President Gordon B. Hinckley at a ceremony at Simpsons Hollow, located just a few miles southwest of Farson. The actions stalled the troops in Wyoming over the winter of 1857-58, giving church and government leaders time to resolve their issues. The troops eventually marched through Salt Lake City and on to a camp southwest of the city without incident.

LDS historian Stanley Kimball, a professor at Southern Illinois University, agreed that the loss of supplies, valued in 1997 dollars at about $4 million, had a telling effect on the episode.

President Hinckley dedicated markers memorializing the Simpsons Hollow events and commended Wyoming Bureau of Land Management officials for outstanding cooperation in a project of mutual interest.

*A ferry specially built to give 1997 trekkers a taste of the challenge embodied in the Green River carries
the Utah state wagon at the historic Lombard Crossing.*

Local Boy Scouts present an array of flags to open ceremonies dedicating markers at Simpsons Hollow. In 1857, a small group of LDS militia destroyed U.S. supply trains at the site. Below, children of the wagon train sing during dedication rites at Simpsons Hollow.

Wyoming BLM Director Al Pierson returned the compliment, saying cooperation between the land agency and local LDS stakes had been outstanding.

A re-enactment of Smith's raid on the supply wagons on a nearby hillside, with smoke bombs to create a taste of authenticity, was watched by several thousand spectators. Among them were many of Lot Smith's descendants, including a grandson, great-grandchildren, great-great-grandchildren and great-great-great-grandchildren. Five members of the newer Smith generations participated as actors in the re-enactment.

Leaving Simpsons Hollow behind, the train continued to the Lombard Crossing of the Green River, where history again was spotlighted. The river, a wide wet ribbon wrapping itself around thousands of miles of western prairie, was like a 20-foot brick wall confronting early pioneers. Crossing it was one of the most dangerous challenges of the trail.

The five official "state" wagons of the re-enactment train were ferried across the Green as a reminder of the perils of that era. "On average, there was a drowning a day," in a period when as many as 50 ferry crossings were dotted along the river, said Terry Del Bene, a BLM archaeologist.

The ferry re-creation included several aspects that were definitely not of pioneer vintage, including heavy tractors on each side of the river to pull the cables that moved the ferry, orange life vests for those on board and a wet-suited Larry Macy of the Sweetwater County Emergency Services Water Rescue Team waiting to dive into the river if a problem arose.

But the mosquitoes were authentic descendants of those that plagued the 1800s pioneers, the wind and blowing dust were the same, and the sense of adventure and danger was real enough.

For Forrest Cramer, the crossing had special meaning. He dropped out of the wagon train for about three weeks to build the ferry used in the operation. After several weeks of changing plans as the Green River fluctuated, sometimes at flood level, the culmination of the event was a relief to him.

Cramer and his hometown LDS ward in Pinesdale, Wyo., donated the ferry to the Wyoming BLM to become part of a permanent exhibit commemorating the dangers of pioneer river crossings.

Six-year-old William Kendell of North Ogden, Utah, finds the rearview vista most intriguing on his sixth day on the wagon trail.

A re-enactment of Lot Smith's raid on U.S. supply wagons included smoke bombs for a bit of realism. Smith's actions helped avert war between the Latter-day Saints and the federal government.

A lot of Lot Smith's descendants participated in Simpsons Hollow re-enactment, including Karl, David, Gary, Mike and Burt (who sported a fake red beard to play the part of his forebear in the dramatization.)

53

Jim Connor of Fruitland, Idaho, has a sunset-colored setting for watering his horse in Groshon Creek at Fort Bridger.

FORT BRIDGER: REST STOP AND HISTORY LESSON THEN AND NOW

The mournful sustained notes of "Taps" ended another day on the trail for the members of the 1997 Mormon Trail Wagon Train re-enactment camped at Fort Bridger, Wyo., on July 9.

Then it was time for a history lesson at the site where the history took place. With wagons and handcarts neatly parked, children fed and dabbling contentedly in Groshon Creek or playing baseball in the grass, adults from the wagon train and interested community residents heard the story of Jim Bridger — trapper, trader and frontier entrepreneur.

Fred R. Gowans, Brigham Young University professor and author of several works on Western history, outlined Bridger's colorful career, which paralleled the opening of the American West. His story also became interwoven with the Latter-day Saint migration to the Salt Lake Valley.

At 16, Bridger was among a group of adventurous young men who answered an ad in a St. Louis newspaper. The ad, placed March 20, 1822, by William Ashley, called for young men to go to the headwaters of the Missouri River to trade and trap. From then until 1840, Bridger followed the fortunes of the fur trade, starting near the Yellowstone River and eventually crossing much of what became the Western states, including Utah. When the fur trade petered out, he established a fort to trade with emigrants on the major Western trails.

In 1847, Brigham Young met Bridger and they discussed the settlement potential of the Salt Lake Valley. Bridger was pessimistic. Based on his intimate knowledge of the valley, he used rocks, sticks and whatever came to hand to create a map more accurate than the one carried by President Young.

By 1855, because of competition and changing migration routes, Bridger was ready to sell the fort to the Mormons. He collected $4,000 — half of the asking price — at the time, and Bridger's partner, Lewis Vasquez, later received the other half during a trip to Salt Lake City.

54

The Latter-day Saints improved the fort and established another, Fort Supply, nearby. In 1857, when U.S. Army troops led by Albert Sidney Johnston headed for Salt Lake City to quell a supposed rebellion among the Saints, both forts were burned to prevent their being used by the Army. When the "Utah War" was successfully averted, Bridger leased his old fort to the military and it was used for a frontier base until 1890.

Regaled with Fort Bridger's history, the wagon train participants settled down for a night in this pleasant camping spot — but not until some of them had danced a few rounds to the fiddle music of Jonathan Dew and the calls of Gus Horn, while the day ebbed from dusk to dark.

July 10, the camp was up early and eager for another day in Fort Bridger. Residents of surrounding communities made it a good one. Plenty of activities kept children and grownups entertained. Youngsters marched from one part of the old parade ground to another, making typical pioneer toys, running three-legged and sack races, winding ribbons around a maypole and generally enjoying a break from the trail.

They continued their play uninterrupted and oblivious of an event unfolding in one of the nearby camp tents. Henry Clarence Bentley was

A weary trekker sheds her shoes and relaxes in the shade of an ancient tree at Fort Bridger.

being born. The baby arrived shortly after his parents, Cliff and Dana Bentley of West Jordan, Utah, drove to Fort Bridger specifically so the baby could arrive in the wagon train encampment.

Utah County midwives Dianna Bjarnson, Gwen Smith, Deborah Aaron and Lisa Heimberger attended the birth in the tent of Shauna Dicken, who arranged it in appreciation of her ancestor, Patty Bartlett Sessions, a pioneer midwife.

In the evening, it was time for another look back to the past. A section of the old wall constructed by Latter-day Saint settlers after the church acquired the property in 1855 was dedicated. The wall, originally part of a large corral, is being uncovered and reconstructed by a group from Western Wyoming College, Rock Springs, Wyo., headed by Dudley Gardner.

Elder J. Kirk Moyes, an Area Authority Seventy assigned to the Utah North Area, dedicated the historic wall as "a monument for us to remind us of this rare occasion." The wall, he said, could represent to the faithful a symbolic hedge to keep bad out and good in.

55

Fort Bridger's creek was an attraction for animals and children. The shady campsite was one of the most pleasant in Wyoming for trail-worn trekkers.

*Above, bouncing along like pint-sized jumping beans,
children enjoyed the old-time sack races during a break in
the trail routine at Fort Bridger.*

56

*Coiled along a dirt trail, the wagon train rolls through
Coyote Creek, outriders keeping a careful watch.*

57

*Linda and Todd Zenger of Salt Lake City made Fort Bridger a stop on a family
vacation so they could absorb some of the wagon train's atmosphere.*

PART FIVE

UTAH:

JOURNEY'S END

For Brigham Young and his company, crossing the Bear River on July 12, 1847, into what became the state of Utah, heralded the beginning of the most difficult part of the Mormon Trail. The thousand miles of prairie behind them could not match the resistance of the mountain range that stood between them and their destination.

Excitement also ran high in the commemorative 1997 wagon train as it filed into Utah somewhere in the unmarked rangeland near Yellow Creek. For these modern pioneers also, the Salt Lake Valley still lay hidden behind the formidable Wasatch Mountains. The most geographically challenging stretches of the trail came in the last few days as high desert terrain gave way first to foothills, then to the steep winding passages of the mountains themselves.

Thousands of awed and enthusiastic well-wishers greeted trekkers in their Utah camps at Castle Rock, Henefer and East Canyon. But the greatest welcome was yet to come. On July 22, thousands lined Emigration Canyon to cheer the trekkers as they toiled off Little Mountain on the last leg of the epic trip. The welcome grew to a roar when the wagon train emerged from the canyon's mouth to a rousing open-arms welcome from an estimated 51,000 people at This Is the Place State Park.

The farewells offered by church and government leaders in Nebraska became the welcome-homes at the trail's terminus in Utah. With mixed emotions, the modern pioneers received the applause of admirers at journey's end, took places of honor in annual Days of '47 celebrations, and then tucked their memories safely away and headed home.

ANTELOPE, CATTLE WATCH AS THE TRAIN ENTERS ITS FINAL STRETCH

The 1997 sesquicentennial Mormon Trail Wagon Train crossed into Utah July 14. Maybe. More or less. Give or take a few hundred feet.

The debate of the day was whether the train was still a couple of hundred feet inside Wyoming, actually across the border or straddling the line. Kids playing in Yellow Creek may have been in Utah while the wagons circled up in Wyoming. It was a close call.

"How could you tell without a survey?" asked Summit County Commission Chairman Sheldon Richins. Ignoring the fine details, he welcomed the train to Utah.

The previous day, official boundaries notwithstanding, Wyoming wagonmaster Ben Kern passed the reins to Utah wagonmaster Bob Lowe during a ceremony at the rodeo grounds in the Wyoming border town of Evanston.

Lowe was already a familiar figure on the trail, his white hair almost disappearing under a hat pulled low against the sun. "I've worked with fine men," he said. "It's not like

After serving as lieutenant through Nebraska and Wyoming, Salt Laker Bob Lowe took over as general when the wagon train entered Utah.

Are we in Utah yet? Precisely where the caravan crossed the Utah/Wyoming border was a much-debated question. But as trekkers passed the Needles area of Wyoming, they knew they were close.

stepping into something cold. We'll continue to work together, but someone has to be the whipping post."

The wagon train participants were guests for the rodeo and midsummer celebration Evanston was throwing. Then, after a night in a gravel pit campground, the camp was on the move again, crossing via highway over the Bear River, then veering off onto rangeland where cattle stopped grazing long enough to watch the wagon train pass by. Several of the animals created temporary diversions as they ran right between wagons to get to the other side.

A herd of antelope also loped single file along the crest of a hill, disturbed by the unaccustomed activity.

"It doesn't get any better than this," said Lowe, but dust soon filled the area as the wagons churned up the rudimentary trail. At times, the trail paralleled ruts ground into the earth by wagon trains of the mid-1800s. They were visible about 50 feet off the route taken by the modern train.

Wagoneers, handcart crews and walkers watched in anticipation as the Needles, a craggy outcrop in the otherwise mostly unbroken line of low hills, appeared. The Needles figured in the journals of some original pioneers. Pinnacles of conglomerate rock, cemented together by hardened silt, the landmark formations were Brigham Young's inspiration for the spires of the Salt Lake Temple, some early writers suggested.

To the left, the snow-topped Uinta Mountains were an indication that if the trekkers weren't in Utah yet, they soon would be.

The train pulled into a campsite near Yellow Creek. A pair of run-away horses, apparently over-eager to get to their feed, ripped around a corner and sent trekkers and visitors scattering while their riders tore

Emptying evening supplies from a wagon was part of 6-year-old Laura Potter's assignment while the wagon train was camped at the red-rock and red-hot Castle Rock site.

along behind — way behind. Someone in the camp managed to catch their reins and stop the runaways. Children tramping the usually clear creek into a mucky mire stopped temporarily to watch the excitement.

The following day there was no longer any doubt. Two Utah state park rangers on horseback were proof positive that the caravan was in the Beehive State.

The trekkers visited Cache Cave briefly, recalling its history as a storage place for fur trappers and then a supply cache for LDS pioneers on the trail. During the "Utah War," the cave was used to stow materials the Utah settlers could use for defense if U.S. Army troops got that far. Echo Canyon was the first line of defense for the settlers, but no hostilities ever occurred.

The trekkers dined royally that evening as guests of the Park City, Utah, LDS Stake, then settled for the night to refresh themselves in anticipation of 24 hot miles down Echo Canyon to Henefer, where a huge celebration was awaiting their arrival.

Ellen Lunt of Farmington, Utah, was waist-deep in desert grasses as she watched the arrival of the wagon train near the Utah boundary.

Into the Utah foothills, the difference was notable. Prairie grasses gave way to sagebrush and pockets of trees.

63

A "kid sandwich" rides through camp at Castle Rock. Laura Anderson is the filling for Todd and Hillary Mellcam.

AT HENEFER, MUSIC FILLS THE AIR

The Hennefer Brothers, James and William, arrived in the Salt Lake Valley in 1850. Three years later, Brigham Young sent them to Echo Canyon to set up a blacksmith shop to repair the wagons of thousands of Latter-day Saints then pouring down the canyon — a pioneer service station of sorts.

The Hennefers stayed and became the nucleus of a little town they called Henneferville.

On July 16, 1997, James' great-grandson, Lehi, and his wife, June, sat on the front porch of their Henefer home (in 1900 town leaders decided to drop one of the "n's" and the "ville") listening to the hoopla of a sesquicentennial celebration and remembering their pioneer past.

It is this "remembrance," Gov. Mike Leavitt told a crowd in Henefer Park, that is the essence of Utah's third jubilee observance. Memories of the past are ties that bind generations and solidify values, he said.

"In every nation, every state, there is an aggregate soul. It is the sense of who we are and what we value," the governor told several thousand people who had come to Henefer to meet the 1997 sesquicentennial

Melissa Jones and daughter, Jennifer, Omaha, Neb., take some play time during Henefer stop to rest up for the serious business of the mountains ahead.

Gov. Mike Leavitt extends an official welcome to Utah during Henefer gala. He lauded the commemorative train as a link with the history and values of the past.

commemorative wagon train. The train's wagons, handcarts and animals were neatly parked in a field bordering the town and were a big draw for the huge crowd that temporarily took over.

It was the train's formal welcome to Utah. Leavitt, who had been out of town when the caravan crossed Utah's border, spent a few minutes before his speech walking through the camp visiting with trekkers.

While their ancestors came by covered wagon, the governor and two other state officials arrived by helicopter. For House Speaker Mel Brown it was a homecoming. He was born in one of the red brick houses in Henefer. Senate President Lane Beattie, West Bountiful, also spoke of pioneer roots.

Leavitt recalled a much-earlier Cedar City, Utah, pioneer celebration when he took off full tilt on his tricycle, which sported crepe paper

65

Day is done. A spectacular Utah sunset backs a resting wagon, but elsewhere in Henefer, a gigantic celebration is under way for the trek's human marchers.

Human brakes strain to keep a handcart in check down a steep hill north of East Canyon reservoir.

decorations and a clacking card attached to the wheels. With his father, former state Sen. Dixie Leavitt, in full pursuit, he outstripped the parade and declared at the end, "I won! I won!" he said.

Henefer Mayor Larry Dearden was seeing the culmination of months of planning. The town of 750 had pulled out all the stops for the sesquicentennial event. The reward was a steady line of parked cars up and down every street and a thriving, temporary, outdoor mall for vendors. Anything cold — shaved ice, soda pop or bottled water — was a going commodity as the temperature hovered near the 100 mark.

To close out the evening, young and old danced in the street to Joe Muscolino's modern music.

The following night was a repeat but with the spotlight on the Utah

Clouds hovering over a toy-like wagon train in East Canyon take on rainbow hues, seeming to promise an end to the journey.

Symphony Orchestra. Kory Katseanes led Utah's premier music contingent through an uncharacteristic program of pioneer-style music, and the wagon train choir joined in for the closing number, "Come, Come, Ye Saints."

Getting the symphony to Henefer was a fluke, Dearden said. He had aspirations but not much hope of persuading the group to come to his small town. Then he just happened to run into assistant symphony conductor Robert Henderson as they both fueled their cars in Salt Lake City. As they paid, Dearden casually asked Henderson if he'd bring the symphony to Henefer. "Sure we will," replied Henderson.

And there they were, lock, stock and saxophone, their music echoing in Echo Canyon.

Wagon train President Brian Hill, sporting "nine new blisters," told the Henefer crowd "what the news media will never report," — that angels traveled with the wagon train. Also on the program was Elder M. Russell Ballard, a member of the Quorum of Twelve and chairman of the LDS Church sesquicentennial events. He proclaimed the 1997 commemorative wagon train "no little thing." Many people, stirred by the modern epic, "paused in their busy schedules to think of their forefathers who struggled to come West," he said.

The frolic in Henefer was the prelude to more serious business — tackling the steep mountain grades that still lay between the wagon train and its destination in the Salt Lake Valley.

67

*The winding roads of East Canyon
had the wagon train coming and going as it strung
out along the switchbacks.*

*Stephanie and Brynn Saetrum, Park City, Utah, give the horses a
handout. The animals were glad for a rest between long hauls in Utah.*

SO NEAR TO THE END, AN ACCIDENT RIPS A WAGON APART

Predictions that June 20 would see the most hazardous segment of the 1,100-mile re-enactment of the Mormon Trail epic came true minutes after the wagon train left an East Canyon encampment.

Fewer than a dozen wagons had filed off the steep incline leading off a plateau before a runaway mule team tore through the brush, leaving the path and heading onto a rocky, uneven area. The wagon the team was pulling bounced hard and flew apart, the bed separating from the axle. One of the wheels rolled into the reservoir at the bottom of the hill.

As the wagon careened down the hill it narrowly missed other vehicles carefully negotiating the grade. The driver was thrown from the box, and five terrified passengers clung on inside. Two eventually were thrown from the rear of the wagon, and the other three stayed inside until the wagon bed bounced to a halt. The team continued a wild run to the bottom of the hill until one of the mules became entangled in the lines and fell, pulling his companion down also.

Aboard were Val Robins, his wife, Gloria; a friend, Kathryn Goodfellow; her granddaughter, Tori, 11; and two additional children, Chase Funk, 12, and Cody Funk, 9, all from Idaho. The Robinses' wagon was the Cassia County, Idaho, entry

A distraught Kathryn Goodfellow is comforted by a friend, Crystal Molen, after being thrown from the runaway wagon.

in the wagon train. Val Robins was treated for a broken arm. Kathryn and Tori Goodfellow were treated for neck pain.

The accident was the second in a short time period. Minutes earlier, the horse team pulling the second wagon in the day's lineup also started off the hill at a run, ramming into the back of the lead wagon, whose driver, Jared Cornell, had his brakes well set when the tongue of the second wagon tore a foot-wide hole in the rear of his vehicle. No injuries resulted.

Wagonmaster Bob Lowe routed the remaining units down another way on a dirt road that had served vehicle traffic into the East Canyon campsite.

It was an inauspicious start to the next-to-last day of travel. But despite the arduous pull up Big Mountain and the steep descent on the other side, no more mishaps marred the day. By evening, separated into two groups to fit into smaller campsites on Little Mountain, the trekkers were beginning to realize that the end was truly in sight.

Anyone who thought the potential for accidents wasn't real was mistaken. When you have that many people and that much livestock in that kind of an environment, your risk for acccidents is very high. The skill levels of the people involved varied greatly, and the chance was always there. It was the reason some of us were a little nervous all the way. The reason we had no more accidents than we did was that we were covered with an umbrella of blessings that protected us.

Bob Lowe, Utah wagonmaster

69

Val Robins' mules take off at a dead run coming off a steep incline above East Canyon Reservoir. As the wagon jolts over uneven ground …

…it begins to separate. Robins has already been thrown off the seat. The disintegration continues as…

… dust clouds kicked up by the careening wagon and team obscure the scene. Fully separated from the wagon bed …

…the mules continue a wild run for the bottom, where one is tangled in the traces and pulls the other one down.

71

Right, Kathryn and Leona Condie of Beaver, Utah, catch a few winks in the family wagon somewhere in Utah. Below, from Henefer to East Canyon Reservoir, the trend is all uphill. The toil up this stretch is to prepare for the higher mountains ahead. Far right, tall trees coating Big Mountain all but obscure the wagon train wending its way through the Wasatch Range. But at the top was the reward — Salt Lake Valley could be seen.

72

At left, even on the trail a lady wants to look her best. Katie Crow stands still while Melanie Bell does a quick "do." Below, from the air, the wagon is a string of beads on the sharp curves coming off Little Mountain.

Aaron Crisp, Napa, Calif., enthusiastically joins the handcart push-pull crews for the last weeks of the trek.

73

THEY CAME OUT OF THE MOUNTAINS AND INTO A ROARING WELCOME

A historic saga that had plucked at the collective heartstrings of people all over the world ended July 22, 1997.

About 11:30 a.m., right on time, the 1997 Sesquicentennial Mormon Trail Wagon Train emerged from the mouth of Emigration Canyon to a tumultuous welcome from admirers and well-wishers.

More than 1,300 miles was under the wheels of a small group that started in 1996 in Iowa. Another 1,100 miles each had been logged by about 220 stalwart "all-the-wayers" who embarked from Omaha, Neb., in April 1997. Thousands more could boast of traveling either a few miles or many miles at some place along the way to Salt Lake City.

From the first blush of dawn, it was a perfect finish to an amazing adventure. As the camp atop Little Mountain roused, a die-hard full moon provided backlighting to clouds that kept the morning somewhat cool. People bustling to complete last-day preparations were aware that any chance meeting might be their last.

"You're welcome at my campfire any time," Utahn Jared Cornell told Ernie West, who had covered the 1,300 miles from Iowa, driving a mismatched team of a horse and a mule.

"This is it," Salt Laker Joseph Johnstun told Kimberli Reynolds of Minneapolis, Minn., as they shared a morning hug.

Utah State School Board member Katherine Garff, who joined the train with her family in Henefer, Utah, called it a "wonderful, wonderful experience," even though a week at a time of riding is not what they're used to.

A trekker slaps his way along Emigration Canyon. Many onlookers hoped for some physical contact with the trekkers they admired.

But with the cloud-shrouded sun topping the mountains, it was time to get down to business. Only a few miles lay between the trekkers and the destination that had beckoned for three months and a day. But the first mile of those few was the worst — a steep, winding descent off Little Mountain before the road gentled off into Emigration Canyon.

It was worth every footstep as the train rolled into the biggest welcome-home party held in Salt Lake City in years. People hung from the windows and lined the patios of high-rise condominiums at the mouth of the canyon to applaud the train. Thousands lined the narrow roadway from the foot of Little Mountain to the canyon egress, shouting, holding up signs, raising hands for a good-natured slap from the marchers, weeping — in general sharing in the emotion of the historic re-enactment.

75

Whoop and holler was the order of the day. A group of young people from the wagon train breaks loose, and flags flying, captures the spirit of the arrival at This is the Place State Park.

Riding abreast, the three state wagonmasters, Joe Vogel of Nebraska, Ben Kern of Wyoming and Bob Lowe of Utah, led the train into the valley for the last few hundred yards amid an ever-increasing din of cheers, applause and shouts. Many greeters waved American flags, and a horse-mounted riding club from Ricks College created a red-white-and-blue splash of color midway down the canyon.

A massive crowd of spectators, held back by mounted police, lined both sides of the path into This Is the Place State Park, where church, government and civic leaders waited to add their formal greetings. A vocalist hailed the arrival with the favorite pioneer hymn,

A tableau of "pioneers" of all ages, dressed in white to represent the 6,000 who died on the trail in the 1800s, touches the heartstrings of modern trekkers.

Several hundred LDS missionaries, bearing the flags of dozens of nations that now host missionaries around the world, line up in ranks near the entrance to This is the Place State Park.

"Come, Come Ye Saints." Several hundred missionaries of the LDS Church, bearing flags from all over the world, represented the growth of the church since its pioneer days. Most touching to many of the wagon train was a tableau of people dressed in white pioneer costumes, standing on the south of the road, portraying the 6,000 Saints who died before reaching the end of their journeys to Zion.

"This is so exciting," said Audrey Lloyd, Salt Lake City. "I wasn't going to come at first. I thought it would be hot and horrible, but then I thought: You can't miss this; this is a once-in-a-lifetime experience." Her sentiments were multiplied by 51,000, the number of people who stood and sat and wilted, all good-naturedly waiting as a formal program unfolded.

76

All three members of the LDS Church First Presidency, President Gordon B. Hinckley and his counselors, President Thomas S. Monson and President James E. Faust, participated.

"You look as if you've come a thousand miles," President Hinckley quipped, then launched into a laudatory welcome. "You have done something really extraordinary. You have caught the imagination of us all. Even to those of you who traveled only a short distance, we owe a debt of gratitude."

He predicted the 1997 commemorative march may be the last of its kind but served to remind the world of the struggles of the original pioneers. As the modern train entered a modern city, it was apparent the desert had, in fact, blossomed like a rose, he said.

The wagon train taught great lessons again of the need for organization and mutual dependence, President Hinckley said, but it also reminded modern admirers of the need to marvel at and appreciate God's creations.

Utah Gov. Mike Leavitt called the sesquicentennial a good time to reflect individually on the depth of commitment and courage felt for and gleaned from the state's pioneer legacy.

Salt Lake Mayor Deedee Corradini recalled that the original settlement created by the pioneers of 1847 was named Great Salt Lake City. "One hundred fifty

More than a thousand miles from his departure in Omaha, handcart captain Mike Dunn, center, leads his troops the last few steps into the park.

Right, President Gordon B. Hinckley, western hat in hand, beams a Salt Lake welcome. Far right, President Hinckley is flanked on his right by his counselors, President Thomas S. Monson and Prsident James E. Faust, and their wives and on his left by Elder M. Russell Ballard, church sesquicentennial chairman, and wife.

years later, and we are still a great city and a great state," she said.

For two more days, the wagon train participants were the toast of the town, traversing the city in its own small parade on July 23 and starring in the annual Days of '47 Parade on July 24th. Many paradegoers, jaded from the hours of waiting and watching, came alive again as the wagon train participants filed along the parade route, hailing the 1997 pioneers.

Then the commemorative wagon train was truly at an end, ready to take its place in history as one of the remarkable events in 150 years of pioneer heritage.

77

Far left, Brigham Young and his early counselors seem to observe in bronze silence from the top of This is the Place Monument as a handcart crew ambles past. Above, Wero Karena and wife, Patsy, celebrate the conclusion of a trek that started — for them — in Hastings, New Zealand. Left, A celebrant gives the universal greeting that was repeated thousands of times.

*Jared and Bre Cornell guide the Utah wagon out of
the mouth of Emigration Canyon while the wagonmasters, right,
ride horseback into the uproarious welcome home.*

79

Left, the combination of tears and smiles was the standard reaction to the culmination of three months on the trail for two young trekkers. Below, Andy Pitcher, Alpine, responds in kind to the greetings of well-wishers.

80

I've learned just how quickly people can pull together. How quickly you can get to know people. How close you can become in such a short time. Also, how you have to rely on each other for a lot of other stuff. And also, the power of God that I've seen in many cases.

Jonathan Dew, Salt Lake City, Utah

On July 24, the wagon train makes a triumphal journey along the annual Days of '47 parade route, one of the country's largest parades, as a huge crowd greeted their final journey with tears and applause.

81

Above, a parade of their own on July 23 saw the wagon train winding through Salt Lake City streets en route to the city's celebration in Washington Square.

Left, the annual Days of '47 Parade was the wagon's last hurrah as a cohesive unit. Thousands of paradegoers expresses appreciation for the accomplishments of the historic caravan.

PART SIX

TRAIL LIFE

TWO WEEKS IN THE LIFE OF A 'PART-OF-THE-WAYER'

By John L. Hart

That magnificent wagon train out of time that crossed half a continent and mesmerized nations is gone now, dissolved into memory as surely as did its predecessor a century and a half ago. And like those wooden-wheeled trains of the original pioneers, it left us powerful mental pictures and stirred our emotions to the depths. No one on the train claimed to be a pioneer — some chasms can't be crossed — but those on the train had profound experiences and gained life friendships.

When I joined the train July 10, the wagons were stopped on the greens of Fort Bridger, Wyo., surrounded by an army of support vehicles, ornamented with children splashing in a small creek.

There on a park lawn next to two mules was my first and best camping place.

Our day began at 4:30 a.m. as motor-wristed Robert Haderle clanged a triangle for about an hour. Thus began the daily routine: feed and water the horses, care for personal needs; at 5:30 a.m., eat breakfast; put away the tent; saddle the horses; go to the 6:30 a.m. camp meeting for a daily briefing, history lesson and prayer; get the horses and be mounted and ready to move by 7 a.m. when the wagons moved out with us at their rear. Midmorning water break and lunch followed. Upon arrival at the campsite, animals were tethered and a two-hour shuttle to the support vehicles and back preceded feeding and watering the stock, supper, pitching tents, evening activities and a 10 p.m. collapse —

Church News writer John Hart learned the wonders and the woes of the trail — including a runaway horse ride — during his two weeks with the wagon train.

followed very shortly by the triangle.

Morning departure was always dramatic. At Fort Bridger, Wyoming wagonmaster Ben Kern yelled something. In a neat line from among the vehicles rolled the wagons, wheels crunching gravel, canvas tops rippling in the breeze. Their teams pranced forward, hungry for the miles that lay ahead. One after another they filed through the fort's parade grounds, grinding to the highway. Lines of spectators applauded.

The Mormon Pioneer Trail out of Fort Bridger leads uphill along pastures toward the railroad ghost town of Piedmont, then across sagebrush flats to the Needles and Yellow Creek and over hills to Utah's Echo Canyon and Henefer.

The second morning, sore and late, I tossed my sleeping bag in the back of the horse trailer and scrambled to catch up. Temperatures hovered in the mid-30s. Breakfast was hurried, and prayer meaningful. Again that morning the wagons put on a show as they circled out of the sagebrush bowl, rocking gently in the pale first light, their drivers and passengers huddled in blankets or coats. On the way out, a team of buckskin mules pulling the big white "people mover" wagon reared in their harnesses and had to be settled.

Dim ruts from the original pioneer trail ran near the road as we reached 7,000 feet-plus altitude. About 10 a.m. an icy wind gusted across the mountain trail — an even grade that once carried Union Pacific rails. Then drops of cold rain began to pelt down. Wind, lightning and thunder amplified the dreary effects. Young riders around us began to shiver. They gathered at the back of a wagon for shelter. Amid the lashing rain they softly sang Primary songs. Soon they were taken aboard Jim Conner's wagon and bundled in blankets.

All my pony wanted to do was put his rear against the storm and shelter his head. Oh, well, some people are like that. Through it all the wagons continued. Horses bowed their necks and walked on. We thought about the pioneers being outdoors all winter.

Finally the rain stopped. The trail descended, joining a paved surface. Here we passed the walkers and handcarts. I remain convinced that these noble, soaked souls, waving flags, swathed in billowing shirts and dresses, could march through Hades and make 25 miles a day. Bless them all.

Here my pony was frightened. If ever there was a concoction designed to scare horses, it is a handcart train. He bolted, and the soaked chin strap on the bridle broke. I might as well have pulled back on a runaway freight train; his metal shoes pounded in a dead run over the pavement.

"Terry!" Like a true Latter-day Saint, I yelled for my home teacher, my source of help in any situation because he is charged by the church to watch out for me. (Terry Schwendiman was on the wagon train, too.) Then the impression came that if I just held on, my pony would eventually stop, which I did and it did.

That afternoon the wagons circled into a sagebrush flat near Bear River. I think it was that day that one of the wagons broke a neck yoke, supporting the wagon tongue. The startled team stampeded down one side of the road and back over to the opposite side, where it was stopped by an outrider. Miraculously, no one was injured.

That night the city of Evanston, Wyo., held festivities for the train with a wonderful Dutch oven supper, words from Gov. Jim Geringer and a free rodeo. For me, my second that day! The Evanston people provided showers and dinners. When you walk into civilization feeling and looking very much like street people from the viaduct, such kindness is

After nearly three months, one young wagon rider might have felt one hill was much like another.

appreciated clear to the bone. My sleeping bag was soaked in the rain, so I crawled into a plastic tarp and put my wet bag over it.

The next morning, July 13, was a welcome Sabbath Day of rest. Services were held in a narrow swale, and people wore their pioneer best. Many visitors came. One older gentleman borrowed our older horse and rode him slowly around the circle of wagons, the two making a twilight team inspecting remnants of a bygone era.

Again, on Monday, the train rolled out at 7 a.m. On this day draft horses churned their great-maned hoofs up an embankment, wood-banging wagons lurching behind. One carriage horse fell and had to be steadied. Down the road, following Coyote Creek, the wagons left pavement for private land and crossed a broad sage plain toward the Needles, jagged spires of rock far from power lines and pavement. Low clouds of dust hung near the wheels as the wagons moved ahead. Ribbed canvas tops formed a long chain; bleached green brush extended from horizon to horizon.

Tuesday, July 15, was the last pristine day on the trail. The wagons again crossed private land, climbing an incline and then at hillcrest, delighting the eye by winding down a ridge. Scrub trees of dark green fringed the two-track dust road, while spread out below waited the orange cliffs of Echo Canyon.

Oddly, the train seemed to move in silence in the dust. A sense of reverence pervaded the re-enactors. We knew the pioneers had been here, that their animals filed along this way much as our animals plodded in the thick dirt, that they were our people and we their descendants who had not forgotten their

toils and pain. We felt, in moments of quietude, deep appreciation for the pioneers. They seemed near at hand; perhaps we felt them watching. It was touching to think that perhaps they, in some small way, appreciated the re-enactment. That day, we "nooned" at Cache (Redden) Cave.

On July 16, we coursed down Echo Canyon. I elected to walk with the handcarts. Roger Holgreen, an "all-the-wayer," let me join in pulling his handcart a ways, along with his sister Lisa and chief cheerleader Ellen Lunt. I manfully pulled the handcart (on paved road) about five miles (mostly downhill). I lasted on my blisters and in extreme heat this day about 16 miles. Then the world started swirling and lights shooting, and I caved into the "sag wagon" with yet deeper appreciation for those among us who enjoy handcarting.

At Henefer my daughter, Lindsey, 10, and my brother, Winston, and his three children joined the train. For wagons, walkers and riders, the trek from East Canyon to Little Mountain was one of the hardest days of all — 24 miles on hot asphalt up and down Big Mountain and up Little

On the trail, duds get dirty. A camper brings in the wash at the Yellow Creek campground before hitting the trail so it can get dirty again.

Mountain. We passed a new team that day that was stopped. One of the dark Belgian horses stood panting with a wet towel on its ears. It died the next day.

At Big Mountain summit, the wagons stopped for a rest break. In the far distance, above the juncture of hazy purple mountains, the valley came to first view. "All-the-wayers" wept at the sight and held prayer. Then they set one rear wagon wheel on "skid," the other on "roll" for stability, readied chock blocks and began the steep descent.

We did not see the wagons descend but saw the silvery skid marks along the switchbacks. On our descent, my brother's big paint reared up on its hind legs and fell backward. I thought it had fallen on my brother's legs, but he'd managed to scramble out as it was falling.

On July 22 we savored every footstep, every horse clip-clop, every wagon rattle, as our historical trail drew to its end. Down off the top of Little Mountain they rolled, muscled haunches of the teams gleaming in the sunlight, wagons rocking to the movement as boats do in gentle seas. At this last leg, eyes were moist at the impending bittersweet completion and goodbyes. Down the canyon quickly — far too quickly — came the train. Then the canyon opened into the valley.

All the people! The brass band! The quiet plodding on the precious few yards of the dusty last two-track, people cheering on each side. Feelings that could be repressed by cold or fatigue but now were surrounded by this kindness found no more barriers. Most everyone wept. My bouncy pony

pranced on, past the international flags representing the post-pioneer flowering of the gospel, past those dressed in white representing pioneers who died along the way. All I could think of was that all of this — the wagon train, handcarts, walkers, riders, leaders, spectators, everyone — was here to honor our valiant pioneers.

We will never know the full extent of the price the pioneers paid, but thank goodness for this united showing of appreciation; how much they deserved it!

Hugs and flowers were part of homecoming. An unidentified young couple has some of each at This is the Place State Park.

87

After a 26-mile day on hot asphalt, a little fiddle music was in order for this unidentified musician at Independence Rock.

Above, thousands of visitors, like these at East Canyon, spent time with the trekkers, sharing vicariously in the adventures of the trail.

Left, sometimes the least popular man in camp, Bob Haderle's job as chief camp jack was to be up first and get the triangle clanging to rouse the rest of the trekkers.

If you haven't a desk, use a bale of hay. Jason Stout, Orem, finds a perch for a session of journal writing.

ACCIDENTS? YES, BUT HEALING TOO

Small accidents occurred daily on the trail. Only a few were serious enough to warrant special medical attention, and trekkers felt priesthood blessings minimized injury and hastened healing. Among those injured:

• A short distance out of Omaha, Leon Harward, Draper, ended up beneath instead of on his horse, Roanie. He was taken to the University of Nebraska Health Center in Fremont, Neb., where X-rays indicated he had a broken collar bone, shoulder blade and rib. Surgery was scheduled, but he left the hospital long enough to inform wagon train leaders of his situation. When he returned to the hospital, doctors were not able to find on re-examination any broken bones.

• Brenda (Bre) Cornell suffered serious injuries near Rock Springs, Wyo. when the mules pulling her wagon spooked and ran. They were traveling through deep ruts and one of the animals fell against the other. As they ran, Cornell was catapulted from the seat and dragged 40 feet. She was taken to a Rock Springs hospital and treated for broken and cracked ribs and a lacerated spleen, but was back with the train after five days.

• Linda Allen, Provo, was a passenger in a wagon driven by Jack Roberts, Provo, when she decided to step out near Fort Bridger, Wyo. As she stepped from the wagon, her leg went numb and she fell, breaking the right femur in four places. She was airlifted to Utah Valley Regional Medical Center in Provo. Several pins and a plate were necessary to repair the damage.

• Jamison King, 3-year-old son of Ken and Pam King, Idaho Falls, was trailing older siblings through the campground near Ogallala, Neb., when he apparently stopped to pet a mule. It kicked him in the face, sending him flying eight to 10 feet. He was not breathing when he landed. Emergency medical technicians immediately gave preliminary aid while an ambulance was sent from Ogallala. Although it appeared he might have serious facial and internal injuries, close examination at the hospital disclosed none.

89

90

Above, on a rest day at East Canyon Reservoir, Tiffany Woods, 10, rests.
The Mesa, Ariz., child then had been on the trail six weeks with her family.
Left, each morning started with prayer. An unidentified young trekker's
face is lost in her devotions. Below, dignitaries made brief visits. Nebraska governor
E. Benjamin Nelson rode a short way with Elders M. Russell Ballard and
Hugh W. Pinnock while the train was in his state.

When the weather turned cool, authentic campers
Mary Lee Jeffs and Cynthia Proud, washing the morning
oatmeal out of a pot, were grateful for real wool capes.

I felt like maybe I could duplicate being
Mary Fielding Smith out here, being a
widow myself. I thought, 'I'm tough. I can
do this.' Then I came out here and was
humbled quickly. It's just a thing you have
to do. You don't know why, but you have
to come out and do it.

Beverly Woods, Mesa, Arizona

91

It wasn't the Virginia reel Boyd Fullmer was dancing, with
his granddaughter as partner. A modern band kicked out another
brand of music in Henefer celebration.

FOR THE CHILDREN, IMAGINATION WAS A WELCOME COMPANION

A popular Latter-day Saint children's song declares that "pioneer children sang as they walked and walked and walked and walked and walked." The littlest pioneers of 1997 also entertained themselves, often in new and unique ways, as they left behind the toys and trappings of their normal lives at home.

At least 25 children, ages 3 to 18, made the entire trip from Omaha, Neb., (Winter Quarters) to Salt Lake City. Hundreds of others, ranging in age from infants to teenagers, spent a day or more on the trail.

Many were like 9-year-old Sarah Kate Sorensen of Salt Lake City, a member of a group from This Is the Place State Park that aimed at an authentic experience. They walked and walked and walked and walked and walked — and loved it. She was unhappy when she was required to ride. Too much of a jostling wagon could become boring.

Very small children found perches in wagons or hung to the waists of horseback riders. When the wagons rolled out in the morning, it wasn't unusual for a child or two to be still sound asleep in their snug mobile beds. A handcart often became a crib when it was naptime.

The bridge over Groshon Creek at Fort Bridger was the perfect place for chucking rocks into the little stream just to hear the plunk.

Bereft of plug-in toys, the little ones had fun stacking rocks, making pictures in the prairie dust, admiring the draft animals and playing with one another.

They wove headbands and bracelets of the stems of prairie flowers, played tag and hide-and-seek. At some of the stops, local hosts had prepared activities especially for the young ones. The children made button spinners, crafted dolls out of squares of cloth with wads of cotton for heads, strung macaroni jewelry and wound ribbons around maypoles. At night, children were among the most enthusiastic dancers when the fiddlers struck up a tune.

Where there was water, there were children. When the "water buffaloes" — huge tanks of water for drinking and giving dusty hands and faces a quick rinse — pulled into camp, they were a magnet for any children close by. Although the water was not to be wasted, more than one taddy was found running it blissfully over blistered feet. When the night camp included a stream, as it did at Fort Bridger, they splashed and plunked rocks to their heart's content.

A bonneted baby enjoying a handcart ride grins at passersby at Martin's Cove.

Ben Sorensen and Robbie Potter knew the ropes by the time they got to East Canyon. They could catch their own necks just about every time.

Language was seldom a barrier for little ones, despite different cultural backgrounds. Yuji Michael Sekiguchi, 9, and his brother Koji Stephen, 6, both of Tokyo, Japan, started the trek from Winter Quarters diffident and shy. Not far into the journey, they had been accepted into full fellowship with the other children and shared equally in the fun and adventure of the trail.

If anything, the children adapted better to the challenges of each day than did the adults. A hay bale was a perfectly comfy napping spot, a tree was good enough for a lounge to loll and write in a journal, and anything that came to hand was magically transformed into an amusement.

For hundreds of modern children whose lives often make no demands on the imagination, the trek was an interlude that will live in memory.

Teenagers, such as Emily Dicken, 13, of Washington found books a good way to pass the hours. She was seldom without one. Sitting to have her hair braided, riding in the back of her family's wagon or resting after the day's march, she tended to have her nose in a book.

Like the pioneer children of the 1800s, many of the wagon train youngsters had responsibilities. Even small children had camp chores. They hauled water, washed dishes, ran errands or pulled sagebrush for campfires at sites where fires were allowed. When tents went up or came down, some were assigned to pull on ropes or help fold canvas.

Paul Merrill, 15, made an Eagle Scout project of creating chicken crates for the trek. Woven of willow sticks tied into tidy boxes, the crates were attached to wagons. A rooster and three hens started the trip. Two of the hens did not make it the whole way. Paul also helped to make a "possum belly" — a tanned cowhide slung loosely under a wagon to store fuel and other items.

Now, that's using your head! William Bryant (Bo) Aimone, 4, had a dip-and-drip approach to the heat while frolicking in Fort Bridger's Groshon Creek.

Right, braids in the morning had generally degenerated into straggly wisps by evening.

93

Quincie Fornelius holds onto sister Lexie, standing their distance to admire a pair of oxen at Henefer. The girls came from Salt Lake City to visit the wagon train.

94

Almost knee-deep in flowers and grasss, Amy Harris is watched over by sister Julie. Children found much to do, despite lack of toys.

Apparently faced with sweeping up the whole desert with a worn-out broom, Morgan Pitcher, 2, registers serious concern.

96

In neon-bright rain gear, the Sekiguchi brothers, Yuji and Koji, blossom where they are planted — in a muddy wet field in Nebraska.

AS BEFORE, ANIMALS CARRIED THE BURDEN AND MADE IT POSSIBLE

How well the pioneers of the 1997 commemorative wagon train fared depended to a large degree on how well their animals fared.

Every day of the three months and one day they were on the trail from Winter Quarters to the Salt Lake Valley, members of the train depended on horses and mules — with a sprinkling of ponies and oxen thrown into the mix — to keep them moving.

Like the pioneers of the 1800s, they were at the mercy of their draft animals. Ensuring plenty of feed and water to keep the animals healthy was a serious concern. Assigned to oversee animal welfare was J.H. Bell (Doc Jim) a Farmington, Utah, veterinarian who also is a member of the board of directors of Mormon Trail Wagon Train — 150 Years Inc., the not-for-profit company that sponsored the train.

Many of the draft animals came from homes where the climate, terrain and feed were different, he said.

Early in the journey, there was an outbreak of pneumonia among the horses. "We had a quick epidemic. Temperatures went up to 104 and 105 degrees. (A horse's normal temperature is slightly higher than a human's.) We started treatment early and kept it up long enough to get rid of the organism causing the problem."

Accidents were inevitable. One horse got caught under a wagon and cut its face, requiring stitches. Another had its leg run

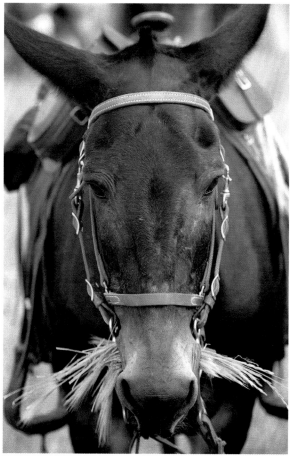

over by a wagon wheel. And several times during the three-month trek, runaways caused problems for animals as well as their human cargo. One draft horse died of exertion shortly before the train reached its destination.

Bell served as midwife to a Schipperkee dog that accompanied a Texas family on the trail. Mariah had five puppies, but one died at birth. The remaining four were sent home to Texas shortly afterward to spare them the hardships of the trail.

A regular on the trek was Bailey, a "one-eyed, bow-legged, gimpy old cow dog" belonging to outrider Danny Van Fleet. The dog spent much of its time in the company of Sue Smith, a trekker from England, who took it along as she walked the trail every day. To taunt Van Fleet, who she said "thinks this is such a macho, tough dog," she bought Bailey a pink collar with "diamond" studs.

The trek coincided with a short feed year in Nebraska and adjoining states, creating a challenge for Ben Kern, Wyoming wagonmaster, who was charged with providing feed. "There's plenty, but it hasn't been the best kind," he said. The animals consumed about 50 bales of hay per day in the early parts of the trip, and the demand increased as wagons and riders joined along the way.

Water was a constant worry. Early on, what was available had a high mineral content that was distasteful for some of the

Hey! Nothing like a little hay to keep a draft horse going. Providing feed for the wagon train animals was an ongoing concern for organizers.

animals. The sheer logistics of getting feed and water to daily camps was amazing, Kern said.

Not all of the animal owners had anticipated the stresses of a long trip, Kern said. Their animals were not prepared, but they toughened up as the train rolled on. His own mules, Kit and Katy, had begun working out six months earlier in anticipation of the trek.

Most of the draft animals were from breeds long accustomed to heavy work — Belgians, Percherons, Clydesdales and Shires. Beautifully matched teams had complementary names — Hank and Eli, Slick and Shy, Seth and Noah, Leo and Louie, Capp and King, etc.

A few oxen were on the trail for short periods. The original pioneers preferred the bulky animals for their staying power, but they were too slow to keep up the pace set by the memorial wagon train.

When the train pulled into This Is the Place State Park July 22, 1997, it was humans who whooped it up in an uproarious celebration, but it was the animals, quietly grazing on the park grounds, that made it possible.

98

Above, chickens far from their usual roost had a temporary home in a cage made of sticks. Two of three hens that began the trip did not make it back home. Left, on a foggy day in Omaha's Miller Park, Carl Jones of Lincoln, Neb., prepares his horses for departure.

Things didn't always go well. Mervin Bennion's horse, April, struggles to get up after a fall in the Nebraska sand hills, but is not injured.

Wagon train veterinarian "Doc Jim" Bell of Farmington, Utah, left, also has time for humans. In this case, his greeting is for fellow Utahn James Arrington, an actor who portrays Brigham Young.

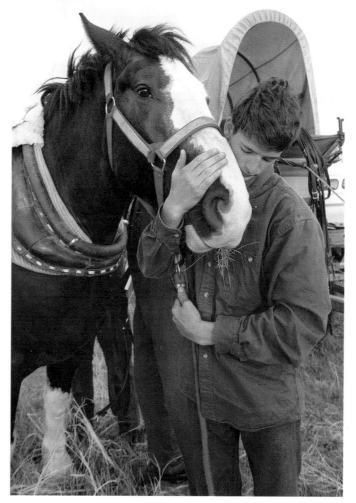

The mutual reliance of people and their animals is evident in John Cornell's loving treatment of a draft horse. The train's well-being depended on the well-being of the animals.

99

Oxen were rare on the trail. Rex Brown, Centerfield, Utah, brought his for a few days.

A TALE OF DETERMINATION WAS TOLD WORLDWIDE BY THE MEDIA

People around the world are endlessly fascinated with the American West and the history of The Church of Jesus Christ of Latter-day Saints. That, coupled with the feeling that this would be one of the last great wagon treks as it covered more than a thousand miles, made the sesquicentennial wagon train a media magnet.

Over the three-month duration of the trek, approximately 120 major news organizations participated directly in the journey or set up long-distance interviews with organizers and trekkers. Dozens of hometown newspapers and television stations along the trail added to the number. At times along the trail, the tricky part of the assignment for many of them was to keep other media out of their shots.

The Public Affairs arm of the LDS Church had expected significant interest in the wagon train and committed a considerable part of its resources to the event. But even seasoned public affairs veterans were surprised at the intensity and scope of the demand. For three months the interest grew beyond all expectations.

ABC, NBC, CBS and Fox television aired reports on the wagon train during popular morning shows. The story appeared on the front pages of the Washington Post and New York Times on the same day. Newsweek and Time magazines devoted space to the saga, and USA Today featured the story prominently.

The Public Affairs Office fielded questions and hosted media representatives from around the world, including Great Britain, Germany, France, Belgium, The Netherlands, the Czech Republic, Hungary, Switzerland, Austria, Romania, Russia,

Italy, Japan and Korea. Two days before the train disbanded, a group from Ecuador arrived as the first contingent from South America.

In the field, traveling by motor home with the wagon train, public affairs missionaries Tom and Sandy Van Leeuwen of Taylorsville, Utah, soon amassed a thick scrapbook of clippings. Every day they filled a variety of media requests from their mobile headquarters, equipped with an array of electronic equipment.

Reporters and cameramen also came carrying the latest in media technology to tell the story of this 1800s re-enactment. Print and electronic reports were available within hours of the events experienced on the long march across America's midsection.

Osamu Sekiguchi arrived in Omaha toting solar panels to capture the sun's energy to charge his battery-powered computers and other equipment. The stories were relayed to two newspapers and two dozen schools in his hometown of Tokyo, Japan. Tucked into the gear bags of the assorted media were the latest digital cameras, laptop computers and an array of electronic gadgetry that fed the appetite of an enthralled public.

One of the most dramatic events of the entire trek happened in a flash as a mule team ran away and wrecked the wagon it pulled just as the train decamped from an East Canyon, Utah, hilltop. Deseret News photographer Jeffrey Allred's sensational photos of the runaway wagon and its six passengers careening down a sage-covered hillside were circulated around the world.

The wagon train story will continue to be told long after the trekkers have settled back into their usual routines at

Utah actor James Arrington, dressed in Brigham Young attire, is used to smiling for the camera. His unidentified little friend needs no practice, obviously.

101

Left, those recording the trek for newspapers and other outlets, such as Osamu Sekiguchi, brought sophisticated equipment then set up on hay bales and other odd places.
Below, at Simpson's Hollow, media wait to capture ceremony dedicating historic markers while the wagon train lines up, off-camera for the moment.

home and the prairie winds have erased the last vestiges of their wagon ruts and footprints.

Gerry Troyna of the British Broadcasting Co. was with the train almost full time after its departure from Omaha, with his son Toby as cameraman. Their long-term observations were to be condensed into a documentary for BBC's religion department in the fall of 1997. National Geographic planned to use snippets from the three-month episode as part of a documentary on population migrations. The program was scheduled to appear in the fall of 1997. The Discovery Channel also expected to air segments for several years after the trek.

In a day when the news tends to dwell on such things as war, gangs, crime, drugs, dissension and dishonesty in and among governments, this was obviously a good-news story that captured the imagination of people everywhere.

TODAY'S WAGON TRAINS DEMAND A LOT OF EXTRA SUPPORT

Providing the daily needs of a moving city with a population fluctuating between a few hundred and almost a thousand people, up to 60 covered wagons, a dozen handcarts and as many as 250 animals daily was no easy task.

The trekkers needed food, potable water, sanitary facilities such as portable toilets, hay and grain for animals, mail service, first aid, an occasional repair job on a wagon or veterinary services, now and then a pair of new shoes and a thousand other unanticipated items. Someone had to follow the train and clean up behind it, seeing that nothing was left to mark its passage.

At every stop along the 1,100-mile trail, the number of motorized vehicles parked somewhere near the wagon train, trying to be inconspicuous, tended to outnumber the animal-drawn vehicles by about 2-to-1.

That's what it took. Along the modern trail, the 1997 trekkers could not feed themselves off the land. Their more touchy stomachs could not handle untreated water from adjacent streams. Landowners and government agencies would not tolerate any lingering reminders of their passage — something with which the pioneers of the 1800s were not concerned. The modern caravan was to leave no traces on the land — only in the hearts and memories of the marchers.

The man behind the support services for the 1997 commemorative wagon train was Leon Wilkinson, a retired Bloomfield, Iowa, educator. In 1996, he

Mail on the trail was delivered by Floyd Hohl of Donnellson, Iowa. He handed out 50 to 150 pieces per day.

made the journey across Iowa, and he remained involved, becoming the operations officer for Mormon Trail Wagon Train — 150 Years.

Bob Haderle, Bradenton, Fla., was hired as chief camp jack, and about 200 people were busy every day with ongoing support services, many of them volunteers or LDS missionary couples.

Even with months of pre-planning, the real thing proved a monumental challenge, Wilkinson said. For instance, the wagon train had to meet the varying health and sanitation standards of the governmental jurisdictions along the way.

The ratio of portable toilets to campers, for instance, had to be regulated according to the number of participants on any given day and the local standards. When the train crossed from Nebraska into Wyoming, the animal feed had to be certified weed-free. Getting adequate good quality hay and grain for the camp's draft animals was a constant concern.

At some campsites, the nearest source of good water was 60 miles away. Huge portable tanks, dubbed "water buffaloes," were in place for the periodic breaks during the day and for the night camp.

For every pair of draft animals providing the wagons with horsepower, there generally was a horse trailer and truck following the line of march, Wilkinson said. At times, as many as 100 horse riders were on the trail besides the wagon riders and walkers, and that meant more horse trailers and trucks to pull them as people came and went.

With the wagon train encountering modern traffic at some locations, safety was an ongoing concern. Local law enforcement officers were recruited to keep the two elements safely apart. Walter Okamoto, a police detective in Syracuse, Utah, traveled with the wagon train most of the time to help with traffic details.

Floyd Hohl of Donnellson, Iowa, was the camp postmaster. Someone had to pick up mail each day from the local post office, and Hohl then delivered it — anywhere from 50 to 150 pieces per day — to trekkers.

The job of feeding the camp was generally allotted to church or community groups along the route. In some areas, private caterers undertook the challenge, never knowing for certain how many unanticipated camp followers and visitors might show up.

The curious mix of roughing it while demanding some of the comforts of modern life made the support role for the 1997 wagon train an unusual but integral one.

Reed Martin, Provo, Utah, ignores the cameraman within elbow's reach as he exults in an exhilerating moment on the trail.

IN SEARCH OF REALISM, THE TRAIN WAS A ROLLING ANTIQUE SHOW

A trip — or many trips — to a neighborhood antique store often preceded the sesquicentennial trip across the plains. People who wanted to replicate as closely as possible the experience of Utah's early pioneers scoured possible sources of authentic equipment to take along.

Some of the more devoted trekkers went the extra mile to make wagons or handcarts based on vintage specifications. A "how-to" booklet, "Pioneer Handcarts," by Stephen Pratt of Pratt Wagon Works, Cove Fort, Utah, became a guide for some. It told how to make an authentic cart "without a particle of iron," as Brigham Young advised in the mid-1850s.

New technology fixes an old wagon for Al Pero, Salt Lake City, Utah. The mix of old and new was a constant feature of the re-enactment.

Many of the wagons that plied the 1997 trail were decorated with wooden water kegs (some paraffin-coated to make them water-tight), iron skillets or huge, heavy cooking cauldrons with tripods to hold them, ancient plows, lanterns, bellows, assorted spare wagon parts, horseshoes and gear and sundry other items to lend a sense of history.

At North Platte, Neb., a replica of the odometer used by Brigham Young's vanguard group of pioneers to measure the distance traveled was installed on the Nebraska wagon to tick off the miles for the modern train.

A bucket of cooking tools is a modern pioneer woman's kitchen-on-the-move.

blossomed each evening. Members of the authentic group also wore clothing that reflected the 1800s. No synthetics for this bunch, just lots of cottons and woolens made from patterns straight out of the earlier era. Before the sewing came the spinning and weaving for some of these intrepid pioneers.

For the rest of the wagon train, equipment was a hodgepodge of everything from antique to state-of-the art. Overall, however, the number of vintage pieces probably was far outstripped by the number of laptop computers and video cameras on this train that overlaid 1997 on 1847.

Left, vintage canteen, bellows and block-and-tackle decorate a wagon. When it came to equipment, the older the better was the idea for many trekkers.

One group on the 1997 trek, sponsored by This Is the Place State Park in Salt Lake City, worked hard at making the camp as close as possible to the real thing. At mealtimes, an old drop-leaf table, several ancient chairs, food storage boxes, spice shelves, heavy bowls and an assortment of authentic cooking utensils came out of storage. A pottery butter churn actually saw service now and then, and the women of the camp found that a scrub board is no substitute for a modern washer and dryer, especially when wind, dust and/or rain left clothing gritty and grimed.

At night, the group pitched white canvas tents that stood out in the little forest of nylon-and-plastic homes-away-from-home that

A wood odometer installed at North Platte, Neb., was a throwback to one designed to keep Brigham Young's company apprised of the distance traveled. Lower left, Joe Sturdy of Oak City, Utah, holds up a wagon tongue while others grease the vehicle's wheels before setting out from Omaha.

A TRAIL LIFE HAS ITS PASSAGES, TOO

Three months is a long time. For those involved in the wagon train, life went on, with the usual passages marked. Birthdays, wedding anniversaries and other personal celebrations either were noted along the trail or put on hold for a more convenient time.

But for some of the trekkers, the trail adventure underscored special life events in a way that will make them long-term conversation pieces.

B.C. Moore and Amy Freestone are likely to tell children and grandchildren that he proposed to her (on one knee, in true romantic style) on the prairie sod somewhere near Keystone, Neb. A horseshoe nail bent into a circle was an appropriate engagement ring, and the rigors of the trail became the traditional test of true love.

Statistically, a fourth of the wagon train participants had birthdays during the three-month journey. Chuck Quillin's 62nd came July 10 as the train was camped in Fort Bridger, Wyo. The day was made special through the generosity of a local woman who learned of the birthday and baked him a cake. It was fashioned like a covered wagon with cookie wheels and had a plastic Woody from "Toy Story" as a starry-eyed teamster.

Mission calls are milestones for Latter-day Saints wherever they occur. Heber Dew's parents of Sandy, Utah, caught up with him near Chimney Rock to

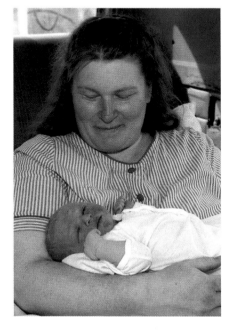

Baby Henry Clarence Bentley, cuddled by mother Dana, was born in a tent at Fort Bridger and blessed in an open-air meeting at East Canyon.

An appropriate birthday cake, a covered wagon with cookie wheels, made Chuck Quillin's 62nd anniversary special.

deliver his call to serve in the North Carolina Charlotte Mission. Lisa Jone Holgreen's call to the California Carlsbad Mission arrived much the same way when her mother, brother and other family members intersected the wagon train near Glenrock, Wyo. Nica Clark got her call to the Canada Calgary Mission at Martin's Cove, Wyo. Jonathan Tyler's brother, Nathan, came home from a mission in Costa Rica and then delivered Jonathan's call (to McAllen, Texas) to the family at Scottsbluff, Neb.

No official "trail babies" were born during the trek, but newborn Henry Clarence Bentley became a symbol for all of those infants who began their lives during the 1800s migration. Shauna Dicken of Plymouth, Wash., one of the long-term trekkers, wanted as genuine an experience as possible. For her, that would mean a birth attended by a midwife, in honor of her great-grandmother Patty Bartlett Sessions, one of early Utah's premier midwives.

Dicken made arrangements with a group of Utah midwives to bring Henry's mother, Dana Bentley of West Jordan, Utah, to Fort Bridger, Wyo., so the baby could be born in Dicken's tent. The birth occurred July 10, less than an hour after the parents arrived in Fort Bridger, and shortly afterward the baby was on his way home to join seven brothers and sisters. To cap the little one's "pioneer story," Henry received his name in a traditional Latter-day Saint infant blessing two weeks later during an open-air sacrament meeting while the train was camped at East Canyon Reservoir in Utah.

At least eight LDS baptisms took place while the train was on the move, including five 8-year-olds of age to receive the customary church rite, and three convert baptisms.

Love blooms on the prairie. B.C. Moore and Amy Freestone courted on the move and became engaged with a horseshoe nail ring to cap their trail experience.

Pulling a handcart 1,100 miles helped prepare Lisa Jone Holgreen, left, for a mission call. Hers, to the California Carlsbad Mission, was delivered in Wyoming.

Near Chimney Rock, Neb., Heber Dew, right, had visitors — his parents, who brought with them his mission call to serve in Charlotte, North Carolina.

108

Being at Martin's Cove and doing Rocky Ridge gives you a much better appreciation for the price that was paid for what we have. Freedom is always bought with a price.

Sherilyn Tyler, Sandy, Utah

There are some thoughts in our hearts. The one thought is that we really wanted to go on this trek for our country, for Austria. We have no pioneers on the plains, crossing the prairie. But we are very, very happy to have the church in Austria, so we are also thinking a lot of the pioneers. There are pioneers in the church, but also in every country, for freedom, if they work for freedom.

Elisabeth Pietsch, Vienna, Austria

People from 11 foreign countries were present at East Canyon. Included are Joel Rohan and Catherine Otterson, Australia; Fredy and Elisabeth Pietsch, Austria; Gleydy DaSilva, Brazil; Harmen Feenstra, Jane, Mathew, Laura, Daniel and Robert Anderson; John and Rose Travers; Rose, Tina, Shelby and Jordan Wraight and Ian Burak, Canada; Sue Smith and Pam Wilkinson, England; Guenter and Christa Liebiech, Germany; Luciano and Mariella Portaluri, Italy; Osamu, Takako, Koji and Yuji Sekiguchi, Japan; Wero, Patsy, Tamaar and Jessica Karena and Emma Archer, New Zealand; Teresa DaSilva and Ana Xarepe, Portugal; Graham and Marion Sully, South Africa.

109

With the journey behind, Larry Turbo Wayne Stewart is baptized in This is the Place State Park mill pond. Elder Hugh W. Pinnock performed the baptism with Gordon Beharrell and Stephen Sorensen as witnesses.

PEOPLE OF THE TRAIL

Ten thousand trekkers, ten thousand stories. Each one who walked a step or a million steps on the Mormon Trail in 1997 had a reason.

Many participated in memory of ancestors who made the same journey in the 1800s. Others were building new "old" memories for themselves and their families. Some came for a taste of America's Western history, others simply to test themselves against the land in an era that offers less opportunity for such tests.

From the oldest (Weldon Beck, 86, of Burley, Idaho) to the youngest (Henry Clarence Bentley, born in a tent at Fort Bridger, Wyo., on July 10) each participant contributed something to the character of the unprecedented modern journey.

Utahns, most with claims to pioneer ancestry, were usually in the majority, but the "all-the-way" list included people from 16 other states and four foreign countries.

Those who traveled farthest to make the complete trip included Fredy and Elisabeth Pietsch, Vienna, Austria; Osamu, Takako, Yuji and Koji Sekiguchi of Nerima, Japan; Gordon Beharrell, Pam Wilkinson and Sue Smith, England; and the Anderson family, Jane, Nathan, Laura, Daniel and Mathew and Jane's father, Harmen Feenstra, all of Balzac, Alberta, Canada.

Short-term trekkers expanded the list of geographic origins significantly. Over the three months of the adventure, representatives of at least 11 foreign countries participated, along with people from every corner of the United States.

Gordon Beharrell's Union Jack was seldom out of his hands. The colorful British flag flapped from Omaha to Salt Lake City whenever the wagon train was on the march, and decorated his small tent when the train was at rest.

Beharrell came from his hometown of Shrewsbury, England, to be part of the commemorative trek as a representative of the many English converts who swelled the immmigrant trains of the 1800s. In particular, he honored the memory of Thomas Davis, the first resident of Shrewsbury to answer the Gospel call on July 28, 1847. Davis was among those Britons who emigrated to join the move to the Salt Lake Valley.

The 1997 pioneer has spent several years involved in researching England's early Latter-day Saints. As a High Council member in Shrewsbury in 1992, he helped develop a "Progeny Identification Program" that attempts to trace descendants of those early church members instead of starting with the current generations and working back.

Beharrell's personal odyssey was not without its challenges. Several months before leaving England for the epic journey from Omaha to Salt Lake City, he underwent surgery for cancer. Nevertheless, he was ready every day to march along with the wagon train, his flag a marker for the handcarts and foot soldiers.

Near Scottsbluff, Neb., Beharrell had a serious setback. He was taken to the Scottsbluff hospital, where surgeons corrected a problem with his colostomy, probably improving his condition overall. When the wagon train marched into Salt Lake City, Beharrell was there, flag still flying.

TREK COSTS

The cost of the wagon train was not insignificant. The estimated price tag — $400,000 — was met through fees paid by participants and a number of contributions.

Some families shouldered the expense of a wagon (the cost greatly multiplied since pioneer days) and draft animals. The "rental" for a space on a wagon was $25 per day. Horse riders paid $15 and walkers $7.50. Meals were an additional $15 per day, and animal owners paid for their feed as well.

After paying all its bills, Mormon Trail Wagon Train — 150 Years, Inc., expected to apply any excess to the preservation of the trail.

The wagon train by all accounts was a marvelous success. Our lives are deeper and richer and we'll be blessed for many years in ways difficult to describe. We now stand as witnesses of the faith and commitment of the early pioneers and of the truth that such faith and commitment still will take a people across the plains.

Brian Hill,
president, Mormon Trails Wagon Train—150 Years, Inc.

Sarah Louise Robinson has her great-great-great-grandmother's name and her spunk.

"She (Sarah Louise Van Orden) did it, and I can do it," said today's Sarah as she started down the Oxbow trail on April 19, 1997 to follow the trail her ancestor had taken almost 150 years earlier.

Robinson was released from the Missouri Indepence Mission of The Church of Jesus Christ of Latter-day Saints just a week before the wagon train left Council Bluffs (historic Kanesville, Iowa) determined that she would walk home. She did it in spite of a congenital condition that causes the muscles in her right foot "not to work well." She had had five surgeries in efforts to correct the problem.

Her slightly gimpy gait became a hallmark for admiration on the trail. Sometimes she had to hitch a ride, but most often she was right in the group of handcart trekkers and walkers, often leading out in a song.

Her assessment of the experience: "Generations that don't remember the lessons of their forebears often must suffer their weaknesses."

Guenter Liebiech had a fascination with old-time wagons many years before he joined The Church of Jesus Christ of Latter-day Saints. During World War II, his mother took her six children out of Germany to Poland and then to Czechoslovakia to escape the conflict. When they returned home, they made the journey in a wagon.

Young Liebiech became a soldier in the German Army and was introduced to the teachings of the church. After four years, he was baptized, along with his wife, Christa, on May 31, 1969. As church members, they became intrigued with the story of the pioneer migration of the mid-1800s and he began to build wagons. Eventually he had eight of them. By profession a sheep rancher, Liebiech found the vehicles useful as well as satisfying his urge to connect with pioneer history.

While he was bishop of the Lauenburg Ward, the ward built a new meetinghouse. On Dec. 11 and 12, 1992, 20 youth and six adults from the ward held a small wagon train journey through the community, camping in bitter cold at the meetinghouse with the wagons circled around the building as part of the dedication observance.

When the Liebiechs learned of the 1997 commemorative wagon train, they decided they had to be part of it. On July 10, they joined the train at Fort Bridger, Wyo. Two of their wagons were shipped to the United States and at Henefer, they joined the company as bona fide wagoneers. A span of red oxen lent authentic charm to their unit, attracting lots of attention during the last week of the trek.

When they returned to Hamburg, Germany, they left the wagons behind, one a donation to the church and the second a gift to a son now living in Seattle.

II3

From Omaha to Salt Lake City, Diana Pitcher took in the sights of the 1997 trek and turned them into sketches and watercolor paintings as part of her personal record of the trail.

At Shelton, Nebraska, townfolk had planted 600 crosses along the train's route, each bearing 10 ribbons to represent the 6,000 pioneers who died in the 1800s Latter-day Saint migration. The scene became Pitcher's first watercolor on the journey, joining the pen-and-ink sketches she had done earlier.

Courthouse and Jail rocks, Fort Caspar, Echo Canyon and other highlights of the trip — a total of 40 different scenes, became part of her watercolor portfolio. She kept three blocks of water color paper rotating in rapid order, two drying while she was doing a painting a day.

For the past 10 years, Pitcher has traveled with her husband, Max, an oil company official. She has filled many "waiting" hours with her artwork, but to now, none may have had as much meaning as those she completed on the memorial trek. She had many requests for copies and hopes to reproduce her trail paintings in some form so she can share the memories.

"Cap"   "King"

Diana Pitcher, Alpine, Utah, turned her impressions along the trail into sketches and water colors, such as the view of a miniature wagon train passing through Echo Canyon, right. The sketch is of Cap and King, draft horses often pulling a wagon driven by Jared Cornell, Salt Lake teamster.

II4

For members of the wagon train's LDS leadership, sabbaths meant putting away dusty clothes and spiffing up in 1800s Sunday attire, complete with tophats.

Mike Dunn, Whittier, Calif., below left, was a counselor to President Brian Hill and captain of the handcart crews that plied the trail. Called as executive secretary was Stephen Sorensen of Salt Lake City, Utah, right. Others in the presidency were Jared Cornell, counselor, and Stewart Glazier, executive secretary.

Dunn was a missionary in the Nebraska Omaha mission while planning for the gigantic 1997 trek was under way and he wanted to be part of it.

He was released from his mission and spent a couple of months at home in Whittier, Calif., before returning to Omaha in April 1997 for the long walk back to Utah.

For many observers, Dunn's group epitomized more than any other the true essence of pioneering. Sometimes the handcarters' enthusiasm carried them right to the front of the wagon train and they would be first in camp.

Sorensen, was part of a group within the 1997 pioneer company that strove to have a genuine pioneer experience. With his wife, Wendy, and children, he and others in their group worked with antique equipment, tents and cooking arrangements to recreate 1800s pioneering as nearly as they could.

The group was made up of This is the Place State Park docents and the makeup rotated among a number of families, but the Sorensens were with the 1997 trek from beginning to end.

Riding into Salt Lake Valley, the 1997 wagonmasters led the caravan three abreast. Each had been lightning rod for the duration of the trek through his own state. From left:

Bob Lowe, Utah. He grew up on a Colorado ranch, served in the U.S. Navy and was a U.S. Department of Agriculture employee for many years before retiring and coming to Utah to found Colorado Stables.

Ben Kern, Wyoming: Also bred to ranching, he worked with his father on the Diamond Cattle Co. He became a trail enthusiast and in 1993 was one of a few who completed the 2,300-mile Oregon Trail by wagon.

Joe Vogel, Nebraska: A 45-year veteran with Union Pacific Railroad, he retired and devoted his time to ranching and guiding trail tours. Tall and lanky, a bean-pole extension of his horse, he was a fixture on the trail.

Right, Russ Leger, Oxbow Trail: A Johnny-Come-Lately to horseriding and trail trekking, he is a former basketball player for the University of Nebraska and long-time businessman. He began following trails in 1993.

Brenda (Bre) Lowe Cornell began to think about a sesquicentennial wagon train years before it became a reality. As a volunteer in the late 1980s at Old Deseret Village in This is the Place State Park, she had the feeling that the village was "Utah's best-kept secret. It had just had a frustratingly slow start."

Working on the contrary theory that "a small problem goes away if you create a bigger problem," she tried to conjure up ways to make Old Deseret a more popular attraction to Utahns and tourists and to "keep Utah's pioneer memory alive." The notion of a sesquicentennial wagon train began to emerge as one way to accomplish the goal.

She broached the idea with her father, Bob Lowe, who later became a concessionaire at This is the State Place Park and created Colorado Stables to facilitate that work. They began to build wagons both to serve the concession and with the growing concept of a wagon train blossoming. Several Colorado Stables wagons were on the trail consistently from Iowa to Utah.

Eventually the entire Lowe family, including the parents and four siblings, was involved in planning and preparing for a trek. Cornell's husband, Jared, was a teamster for most of the distance, from Nauvoo to Salt lake City.

As the plan began to unfold in Utah, it paralleled activities in Iowa where a couple of wagon train groups had decided to commemorate the 1996 150th anniversary of the Latter-day Saint march across that state.

The Utah group began to communicate with the Iowa groups, and a growth of "serendipity and synergy" developed, she said. The wisdom of a combined effort from Winter Quarters to Utah in 1997 became apparent.

"Sometimes things didn't go well," she said. The urgency of a thousand details provided opportunity for disagreement and different opinions among the dozens who ultimately were inolved. On April 21, the dream of a wagon train became a wagon train in fact.

Somewhere along the trail, the train "took on a life of its own," Bre Cornell recalls. She credits the constant infusion of fresh short-termers who spread the word. By the time the train hit the Nebraska/Wyoming border, it was a phenomenon capturing the imagination of people around the world.

From her own perspective: "I'm grateful to have been a part of it. I was only a tool in the hands of something bigger." The thousands of lives that were touched made it all worthwhile.

Alfred (Fredy) and Elisabeth Pietsch of Vienna, Austria, fulfilled a pilgrimage in the 1997 trek. They are pioneers in their own right, both the first in their families to become members of the LDS Church.

"Austria is my home and I love it. But Utah is my spiritual home," said Mrs. Pietsch when the wagon train was approaching the Utah border. She tearfully made the crossing and tearfully celebrated when the train made its entry into This is the Place State Park.

The sacrifices of the early Mormon pioneers made the church in Vienna possible, she said. They are members of the Vienna 1st Ward. Fredy Pietsch, a retired banker and 71 years old, often was off and away down the trail before the wagons, handcarts and other walkers were out of camp in the morning. Despite some periodic illness, he was one of the faithful foot soldiers who seldom missed a beat through the three months of the trek.

The Pietsch's Austrian flag, attached to the Utah wagon, was fairly well tattered by the time Utah was in sight, but they were determined that it would complete the journey to the final destination. And it did.

Larry Turbo Wayne Stewart was a popular fixture on the trail from Nauvoo to Salt Lake City. His infectious enthusiasm grew out of an appetite for adventure, although he had no LDS pioneer ancestry of his own to spur his participation in an event commemorating the pioneer journeys.

In a short lifetime he had been a rodeo clown, a race car enthusiast and trainer of exotic animals. He adopted the nickname "Turbo" and later had it legally made a part of his name.

What began as an adventure for the 25-year-old ended on a religious plane. As the train journeyed across nearly 1,400 miles, he began to observe special blessings given to ill or injured LDS members of the company. He began to study the Gospel and on July 22, 1997 — the day the wagon train arrived in Salt Lake City — he was baptized a member of the church.

The ceremony was performed in a mill pond at This is the Place State Park by Elder Hugh W. Pinnock of the First Quorum of the Seventy, with several hundred wagon train members and other interested onlookers in reverent attendance.

En route back to Milton, Ia., Stewart suffered a serious accident near Rock Springs, Wyo., on Aug. 2, 1997. While he loaded his wagon onto a flatbed truck, the wagon broke loose, rolled and pinned him between the wagon and a van, inflicting critical head injuries.

Dozens of his wagon train companions and other well-wishers flooded LDS Hospital in Salt Lake City with calls inquiring about his condition. Many contributed to a fund administered by Zions Bank to help meet the costs of his hospitalization.

One of his fellow trekkers, Russ Leger of Plattsmouth, Neb., went the extra mile — many extra miles — to assist Stewart. By the end of August, Leger was headed back on the long, long trail to Salt Lake City, raising money to help offset Stewart's enormous medical bills. He was asking for time on local radio stations, meeting with town groups, talking with individuals — anything he could do to help build the Zions Bank account.

Meanwhile, after several weeks of intensive treatment for brain trauma, Stewart had not regained consciousness, although he was in stable condition. His mother, Connie, then arranged to have him flown to the University of Iowa Hospital in Iowa City.

"I don't know if he can recover, but he has a strong will and we (hope that he can,)" she said. Stewart left Salt Lake City with the best wishes and ongoing concern of many wagon train members who came to admire the young man during their trail time together.

F*rom Salt lake City to Tokyo, from Cape Town, South Africa to Samoa, members of the worldwide church have rallied to pay tribute not only to our unique pioneer heritage but to church pioneers everywhere. Whether seen through millions of hours of community service, through the wagon train that wound its way across a thousand miles or through the spectacular celebrations at Brigham Young University's stadium, 1997 will stand as our heartfelt tribute to the heroic sacrifices of all those who have gone before.*

Elder M. Russell Ballard,
member of the Quorum of the Twelve and chairman
of the church sesquicentennial committee

117

EPILOGUE

REPETITION AND REMEMBRANCE

By Edward A. Geary

Director, Charles Redd Center for Western Studies
Brigham Young University

When the first company of Mormon pioneers entered the Salt Lake Valley in 1847, they knew they had achieved something of historic importance. On July 26, only two days after his arrival, Brigham Young, still weak from the effects of "mountain fever," led a small party to the top of Ensign Peak where they planted a flag as a symbolic "ensign to the nations." It marked the place of gathering to which almost 70,000 Latter-day Saints would come before the completion of the railroad. But even the far-seeing Brigham Young might not have anticipated the intense interest stimulated by the sesquicentennial re-enactment of the pioneer trek during the spring and summer of 1997. In addition to the hardy group who followed the entire trail from the banks of the Missouri to the valleys of the mountains, as many as 10,000 others joined the excursion at one point or another, if only to walk a few yards in the footsteps of the pioneers. An estimated 50,000 turned out to welcome the travelers to the valley. Many more thousands, perhaps millions, followed media reports of the trek. The sesquicentennial re-enactment was clearly one of the major events in America during 1997 and attracted considerable attention throughout the world.

How are we to account for the breadth and depth of interest generated by this event? What impelled participants to spend several months amid the mud, dust, heat and general discomfort of the trail? What led so many others to follow so attentively the participants' daily activities and minor triumphs and disasters?

A cynic might suggest that the public fascination was a product of media attention, rather than an occasion, but there was clearly more to it than that. The Great Trek had great appeal simply as an adventure. To travel by foot and animal-drawn vehicles across a good portion of this large continent is an opportunity few can hope to have at the end of the 20th century — and perhaps an opportunity that will never again be possible on so ambitious a scale. Beyond the adventure motive, some participants and observers were inspired by a desire to draw closer to pioneer ancestors through a direct or vicarious repetition of their experiences.

For others the trek represented a chance to claim a heritage they have adopted by choice rather than by ancestry, as was demonstrated most poignantly by the Russian Latter-day Saints who participated at a distance by pulling a handcart across Siberia.

The sesquicentennial re-enactment added yet another layer of significance to what was already a cultural icon: the trail and its trials. As Wallace Stegner observed more than thirty years ago, "the stylized memory of the trail" is "close to the heart of Mormondom":

For every early Saint, crossing the plains to Zion in the Valleys of the Mountains was not merely a journey but a rite of passage, the final, devoted, enduring act that brought one into the Kingdom. Until the railroad made the journey too easy, and until new generations born in the valley began to outnumber the immigrant Saints, the shared experience of the trail was a bond that reinforced the bonds of the faith; and to successive generations who did not personally experience it, it has continued to have sanctity as legend and myth. (1)

The pioneer trek evokes some mythic archetypes that are deeply meaningful in human experience: the journey, the quest, the pilgrimage. And as with all myths, repetition and ritual play an important role in keeping the meaning alive through successive generations. Even the original pioneer trek was in some ways a re-enactment. Participants carried with them the memories of earlier forced migrations, from New York to Ohio, from Ohio to Missouri, from Missouri to Illinois. Then there were the scriptural antecedents. The pioneers deliberately invoked the model of the biblical exodus, organizing themselves as "the camp of Israel" with "the American Moses," Brigham Young, at their head. Also present to their minds were the flight of Lehi into the wilderness and other religion-motivated journeys recorded in the Book of Mormon.

Furthermore, the original trek was repeated again and again as other companies followed the trail across the plains and as settlers were sent out from Salt Lake Valley to colonize more remote and often more difficult places. Indeed, as historian Charles S. Peterson has noted, Salt Lake City and nearby areas passed though the pioneering phase within a relatively short time, and "the hinterland, where the process of the call, the trek, and the establishment of the village repeated itself, became the bulwark of Mormonism in its most distinct form" (2).

After all the habitable areas had been colonized, actual repetitions of the pioneer trek gave way to symbolic re-enactments. The jubilee commemorations of 1897 and 1922 and the 1947 centennial were given special emphasis, but annual Pioneer Day celebrations have been a fundamental part of the fabric of life in Mormon country, where July 24th rivals July Fourth as a patriotic holiday. My own vision of the pioneers was shaped not only by the family stories recounted by my grandparents, but by our small-town July 24th parades, invariably led by a man costumed and bearded to represent Brigham Young, and always including a covered wagon or two, a handcart, a hayrack garnished with sagebrush and carrying women in pioneer dresses and poke bonnets seated at a spinning wheel, and (looking to the future as well as the past) another hayrack crammed full of children and bearing the perennial banner "Utah's Best Crop." In later years I observed my own children's pleasure in the simple parade arranged each year by our LDS ward Primary organization. They preferred dressing up and riding their tricycles or pulling a wagon around the church parking lot to watching the big Salt Lake parade on television. And rightly so, for it is in repeating the trek, on however small a scale, that we draw nearest to the meaning of the original event.

The memory of the pioneer trek has also been kept alive in LDS pulpit rhetoric, serving as a reservoir of images illustrating fortitude in the face of life's challenges, going forward despite painful losses, and the necessity of sacrificing worldly possessions in order to "lighten the load" for the difficult passage ahead. The rescue of the Martin and Willey handcart companies has provided an effective metaphor for "bringing in from the plains" the burdened, the troubled, or the straying. As Stegner observed, "the hard trail was both religiously and artistically right: a labor to be performed, difficulties to be overcome, dangers to be faced, faithfulness to be proved, a great safety to be won" (3).

Historians tend to regard such events as the Great Trek of 1997 with some ambivalence. On the one hand, they are effective in stimulating interest in the past and its continuing relevance for the present and future. On the other hand, however, they are essentially costume drama and provide only limited and generally superficial insights into the actual historic events. It is, of course, impossible at the end of the 20th century to recreate the actual conditions of travel into the American wilderness of 1847. The original pioneers had no support vehicles accompanying their wagon train, few if any sources of resupply along the trail, nowhere to turn in case of emergency except to their own skills and their faith. Wisely, organizers of the commemorative trek did not aim at a strict authenticity.

Ox teams had only a slight role in the 1997 event, even though they were the predominant draft animals for the pioneers. But working oxen are much harder to find today than horses. Furthermore, oxen were regarded as being too slow for use in the re-enactment. There were no handcarts in the original pioneer company, but they were featured prominently in the 1997 trek (and on the official "Faith in Every Footstep" logo), probably because they symbolize pioneering at its most arduous. Despite our reverence for our pioneer forebears, most Mormons have a rather uncertain grasp of history. The sesquicentennial events will do little to dispel the popular notion that everything happened at more or less the same time: the original trek, the rescue of the handcart companies, the invasion of Johnston's Army, the miracle of the seagulls. Indeed, commemorative celebrations probably reveal more about contemporary interests and concerns than they do about the historical events being commemorated.

If the sesquicentennial celebration as a whole did little to encourage a critical understanding of historic events, that was not its main purpose. Historic legends are as important to the vitality of a living society as historic facts — probably more important. The poet T.S. Eliot wrote that "as one becomes older ... the past has another pattern, and ceases to be a mere sequence — or even development." He added, "A people without history is not redeemed from time, for history is a pattern of timeless moments" (4). The pilgrimage of the Mormon pioneers across the Great Plains to the Valleys of the Mountains is such a timeless moment, still deeply meaningful to Latter-day Saints even though a majority of Church members now have no family links to the Utah pioneers, still capable of inspiring even those with no connection to the LDS Church.

1. Wallace Stegner, *The Gathering of Zion: The Story of the Mormon Trail* (New York: McGraw Hill, 1964), 1.
2. Charles S. Peterson, *Utah: A Bicentennial History* (New York: W. W. Norton, 1977), 40, 41.
3. Stegner, *Gathering of Zion,* 3.
4. T. S. Eliot, *Four Quartets* (New York: Harcourt, Brace, and World, 1971), 39, 58.

ACKNOWLEDGMENTS

The decision to produce this book arrived at about the time the Mormon Trail Sesquicentennial Wagon Train was entering Utah and headed for its tumultuous welcome. A little over a month later, the book was ready for printing. A great many people made such quick production possible. Acknowledging all of them isn't possible, but special thanks should go to L. Glen Snarr, Deseret News chairman of the board, and John Hughes, editor, for their enthusiastic commitment to the project. The Church News contributed not only stories and photographs from the Nauvoo and Iowa portions, but Dell Van Orden, its editor, was invaluable help in critically reading the copy. The art and photography departments doubled up on their regular work to free Stephanie Tanner-Brown, Heather Tuttle and Jeffrey Allred for their outstanding production work. Twila Van Leer is supposed to be retired after a stellar career at the paper, but she worked as hard as anyone, not only reporting on the trail but also writing and rewriting stories for the book. All worked late into the night to make the book's deadlines.

Our marketing director, Steve Handy, guided us skillfully through the intricacies of book publishing. We are also grateful for the help and advice given us by individuals from the wagon train, who cheerfully offered valuable insights into their journey. Photographs of Wagon Train participants are used pursuant to license from Mormon Trail Wagon Train — 150 Years, Inc. Our thanks to Ted Wiggins of Wiggins Production Management for his guidance and to Publishers Press of Salt Lake City for making press time available.

—Don C. Woodward

Additional copies of this book may be ordered from theDeseret News, Box 1257, Salt Lake City, UT, 84110, for $12.45, which includes shipping and handling. It may also be ordered over the Internet at www.desnews.com

EDITOR

Don C. Woodward

WRITERS

Twila Van leer
John Hart
Dell Van Orden
R. Scott Lloyd
Gerry Avant

PHOTOGRAPHY

Deseret News Staff

Jeffrey D. Allred
Gerry Avant
Garry Bryant
Laurel Caryn
John Hart
R. Scott Lloyd
Gary McKellar
Laura Seitz

Tom Smart
Twila Van Leer
Dell Van Orden
Chuck Wing

Others

Welden Andersen
Ray Longhurst
Ray Paskett
Lisa Reinert

PRODUCTION

Art direction and design, Stephanie Tanner-Brown
Additional layout and production, Heather L. Tuttle
Map, inside cover: Craig Holyoak

THE DESERET NEWS

Wm. James Mortimer, publisher
John Hughes, editor
Steve Handy, marketing director

All of the photographs in this book are by Deseret News staff photographer **Jeffrey D. Allred,** *with the following exceptions listed by page:* **Welden C. Andersen** *109, 112,* ©*1997 The Church of Jesus Christ of Latter-day Saints. Used by permission.* **Gerry Avant** *44;* **Garry Bryant** *15, 17, 18, 20, 21, 22, 23, 24, 25;* **Laurel Caryn** *88, 93, 95;* **John Hart** *60, 62, 85, 86, 104;* **R. Scott Lloyd** *6, 8, 9, 19;* **Ray Longhurst** *10, 11, 12, 13;* **Gary McKellar** *64, 65, 91;* **Dell Van Orden** *22, 24, 90;* **Ray Paskett** *114;* **Lisa Reinert** *115;* **Laura Seitz** *1, 42, 56, 60, 118;* **Tom Smart** *61, 63, 84, 90;* **Twila Van Leer** *88, 92, 115, 116;* **and Chuck Wing** *78, 79, 90.*

Twila Van Leer and Jeffrey D. Allred

Section Front photography

Foreword: *At rest for the night, a wagon catches the last rays of a setting sun in Fort Bridger, Wyo.*

Introduction: *A Fort Bridger creek was too tempting for Hailey Ricks, Jackson, Wyoming, to resist. Each individual on the 1997 Sesquicentennial trail re-enactment found his own pleasures and pains in the three-month trek.*

Nauvoo, page 7: *A setting winter sun seems to beckon wagons west. In February 1996, the wagons represented the beginning of the epic Mormon journey from Nauvoo to the Rocky Mountains.*

Iowa, page 15: *Russ Leger, Iowa trails enthusiast, watches from a grassy knoll as the 1996 re-enactment caravan passes through a section of southwest Iowa en route to Council Bluffs.*

Nebraska, page 27: *A group of handcart trekkers put their backs into the effort of getting their vehicles up a gentle, sandy slope in central Nebraska.*

Wyo, page 43: *Snaking its way through southern Wyoming rangeland, the wagon train had definitely left the prairie and moved into desert sage.*

Utah, page 58: *The Utah state wagon, driven by Jared Cornell, led the train into Salt Lake Valley to a riotous welcome from thousands at This is the Place State Park.*

Trail life, page 82: *After a daunting day, the dance. At Fort Bridger, trekkers enjoyed the last moments of daylight dancing on the grass.*

People of the Trail, page 110: *Skirts hoisted daintily, modern pioneers Amee Olsen, Darla Jones, Angelene Israelsen, Angie Olsen and Devarie Jones wade through cool Groshon Creek.*

Epilogue, page 118: *Dust dims the trail through Wyoming.* **Page 125:** *The rising sun attempts to shine through fog in an Omaha park, where trekkers prepared for their leave-taking in mid-April, 1997.*

123

Although 10,000 people took part in the 1997 re-enactment of the 1847 trek along the Mormon Trail, relatively few were on the trail from beginning to end. This list provided by officials of the wagon train includes those who left Omaha, Neb., on April 21 and were still with the group when it arrived in the Salt Lake Valley on July 22. Members of a smaller group that also crossed Iowa the preceding year as part of the 1996 sesquicentennial observance are noted by asterisks.

Adams, Jackie and Nance *Pine, Colo.; walkers*
Aldrich, Angela *Meridian, Idaho; teamster*
Anderson, Jane, Nathan, Laura, Daniel and Mathew
    Balzac, Alberta, Canada; wagon riders
Beck, J. Weldon *Burley, Idaho; horse rider*
Beharrell, Gordon *Shrewsbury, England; walker*
Bennett, Alex *Lincoln, Neb.; walker*
Bennion, Mervin, *West Jordan, Utah; teamster*
Boas, Tom and Mary *Bloomfield, Iowa; teamsters**
Bodily, Amy *Manhattan, Kan.; walker*
Brighton, Max and Miriam, *Idaho Falls, Idaho; teamsters*
Clark, Margaret *Cedar City, Utah; walker and Internet writer*
Condie, Vernon and Carol *Beaver, Utah; teamsters*
Daugs, Naomi *Logan, Utah; walker*
Dew, Heber *Sandy, Utah; walker*
Dew, Jonathan *Salt Lake City, Utah; walker*
Dicken, Shauna, Jennifer, Emily, Christina and Sarah
    Plymouth, Wash.; teamsters
Dunn, Michael *Whittier, Calif.; handcart captain*
Ellis, Steve *Provo, Utah; horse rider*
Faerber, Dave *Kaysville, Utah; teamster*
Fairbourn, James *Provo, Utah; outrider*
Feenstra, Harmen *Balzac, Alberta, Canada; teamster*
Fielding, Marion (Pat) *Summerville, Ore.; teamster*
Flake, Sanford and Louise *Snowflake, Ariz.; horse riders*
Freestone, Amy *Orem, Utah; walker*
Gines, Dale and Linda *Hanna, Utah; teamsters*
Goodfellow, Richard and Kathryn *Burley, Idaho; horse riders*
Hailey, Ray and Pat *New Virginia, Iowa; teamsters**
Hazlett, Dean, Carol, Jason and Hannah Meyer *Buffalo,*
    Wyo.; teamsters*
Herterich, Kimberly, Adrianna, Jeremiah, Rebekah and
    Orrin *Hemmet, Calif.; walkers*
Hohl, Floyd *Donnellson, Iowa; teamster**
Holgreen, Roger and Lisa *Bountiful, Utah; walkers*
Hughes, Brent *Mesquite, Nev.; horse rider*
Johnson, Bob *Orderville, Utah; walker*
Johnstun, Joseph *Salt Lake City, Utah; walker**
Jones, Carl *Lincoln, Neb.; teamster*
Kern, Ben *Evansville, Wyo.; teamster, Wyoming*
    wagonmaster*

King, Joseph *Orem, Utah; walker*
Laws, Doug *Des Plaines, Ill.; walker*
Leger, Russ *Plattsmouth, Neb.; Oxbow wagonmaster**
Lewis, Shalisse *Sandy, Utah; walker*
Lloyd, Kimberly *Fremont, Calif.; walker*
Lodefink, John *Magna, Utah; walker*
Madsen, Dan *Delta, Utah; outrider*
Marincic, Don *Big Piney, Wyo.; teamster*
Masters, Cecily *Macon, Mo.; wagon rider*
McCormick, Doris *East Peoria, Ill.; outrider*
Merrill, Paul, **Bonnie, Keith and Shawn** *Orem, Utah;*
    wagon riders
Moore, Brent C *Scottsdale, Ariz.; walker*
Moore, Ted *Marshfield, Mo.; walker*
Nelson, Glen, Janet and Zach *Atlantic, Iowa; teamsters**
Olsen, Dahl *Mesquite, Nev.; teamster*
Orchard, Esther *Richmond, Ky.; horse rider**
Orchard, Latoya *Carey, Idaho; horse rider*
Otterson, Catherine *Farmington, Utah; walker*
Packard, Grant *San Luis Obispo, Calif.; walker*
Pero, Allyn, *Salt Lake City, Utah, teamster*
Petramalo, Gilbert (Pete) and Gretchen, Joseph
    Petramalo and Joseph Flake, grandsons *walkers*
Pietsch, Fredy and Elisabeth *Vienna, Austria; wagon*
    riders, walkers
Pitcher, Max and Diana *Alpine, Utah; teamsters*
Proud, Julie, Amy, Elizabeth and Cindy *Taylorsville,*
    Utah; walkers
Quillin, Chuck and Mary *New Sharon, Iowa; teamsters**
Rasmussen, Milton *Kennewick, Wash.; teamster*
Roberts, Jack *Provo, Utah; teamster*
Robertson, Dean and Donna *Idaho Falls, Idaho; teamsters*
Robins, Val and Gloria *Burley, Idaho; teamsters*
Robinson, Sarah *West Jordan, Utah; walker*
Rowland, Glen, Margaret and Stephanie *Spanish Fork,*
    Utah; walkers
Schwartzkopf, Dale *Clinton, Iowa; horse rider**
Scott, Wayne *Farmington, Utah; teamster*
Sekiguchi, Osamu, Takako, Yuji and Koji *Tokyo, Japan;*
    wagon riders
Silsby, Jim and Josh *Lamoni, Iowa; teamsters**
Smith, Heidi *Salt Lake City, Utah; walker*
Smith, Sue *Shifnal, England; walker**
Sorensen, Stephen, Wendy, Ben, Sarah, Peter and Libbi
    Salt Lake City, Utah; "authentic camp"
Starling, Virginia and Kimberly *St. George, Utah; walkers*
Stewart, John (Tennessee John) *Knoxville, Tenn.; teamster*
Stewart, Larry Turbo *Milton, Iowa; teamster**
Stickel, Kathy *Huntington Beach, Calif.; walker*
Sturdy, Joe and Pat *Oak City, Utah; teamsters*
Taylor, John *Pasco, Wash.; horse rider*

Thurston, Ferris and Anita *Brigham City, Utah; teamsters*
Tyler, Sherilyn, Jonathan and Crystal *Sandy, Utah; walkers*
Van Fleet, Danny *Dallas City, Ill.; outrider**
Vogel, Joe and Donna Clark (granddaughter)
    Red Cloud, Neb.; Nebraska wagonmaster
Wells, Cindy, Elizabeth and Jennie *Merino, Colo.; walkers*
West, Ernie *Clinton, Iowa; teamster**
Whittaker, Tom, Linda, Ryan, Brent, Daniel and Aleah
    Midway, Utah; teamsters*
Wilkinson, Pam *Shropshire, England; walker*
Wilson, Carli *Temecula, Calif.; walker*

Officers of the wagon train and support personnel who made the entire trip include:
Bell, Jim and Eileen *Farmington, Utah; (Jim)*
    veterinarian and wagon train trustee*
Cornell, Jared, Bre and John *Salt Lake City, Utah; (Bre)*
    wagon train trustee
Cunningham, Richard and Erma *Bountiful, Utah;*
    family history missionaries
England, Larry *Bloomfield, Iowa; concessionnaire**
Haderle, Bob and Mary *Bradenton, Fla.; head camp jacks**
Hill, Brian, Karen, Les, Leezanna, Mariah and Kalli
    Kearney, Neb.; (Brian) company president
Irving, Jolene, Jacob, Michael, Melissa, Sarah, Amy,
    Alison *Houston, Tex.; staff*
Jenkins, Richard and Lorraine *Fruitland, Idaho; camp jacks*
Lowe, Bob and Sarah *Salt Lake City, Utah; (Bob)*
    wagon train trustee and Utah wagonmaster
Lyons, Jess *Rigby, Idaho; camp jack*
Merrill, Burt and Lola *St. David, Ariz.; family history*
    missionaries
Molen, Crystal, LeeAnna and Kevin *Houston, Tex.; staff*
Pierce, Jerry and Jan *Taylorsville, Utah; registration*
Toone, Jury and Marjean *Bountiful, Utah; concession*
    missionaries
VanLeeuwen, Tom and Sandy *Taylorsville, Utah;*
    public affairs missionaries
Westergard, Wendy *Salt Lake City, Utah; staff*
Wilkinson, Leon and Judy *Bloomfield, Iowa; (Leon)*
    wagon train trustee, operations director*

An Odyssey group recording the adventure also traveled all the way with the wagon train, including:
Ballard, Michael, Jennifer and Gina *American Fork, Utah*
Bridgers, Courtney *Goleta, Calif.*
Goodman, Kels *South Padre Island, Texas*
Mitchell, Kevin *Orem, Utah*
Newbold, Bruce *Downey, Calif.*
Pack, Brody *Alpine, Utah.*